Orwellian Language and
the Media

Orwellian Language and
the Media

PAUL CHILTON

Pluto Press

First published 1988 by Pluto Press
11–21 Northdown Street, London N1 9BN

Copyright © Paul Chilton 1988

Typeset by Wordbook Ltd, London
Printed and bound in Hungary

British Library Cataloguing in Publication Data

Chilton, Paul
  Orwellian language and the media.
  1. Language—Political aspects.
  I. Title
  401'.9   P95.8

  ISBN 0–7453–0173–8

Contents

Preface

This collection of essays derives from papers, talks and articles prepared during the period from 1981 to 1985, usually at the request of others – linguists, journalists, peace organisations – who thought there was something to say about the role of language in the moulding of public opinion. The chapters of this book, therefore, have a common origin in a common concern. They are not the end-product of an academic programme, but a rational (I hope) attempt to make some sense of questions that were of concern to many people as the 1980s began. To that extent, they leave the way open for more questions and more, and better, answers.

Some questions came mainly from the left, some from the not-so-left. Granted the material effects of the military, the economic and the political, how had the electorate of a democracy (in which ideas and facts were supposed to be freely communicated) been persuaded to accept the escalator of nuclear insecurity? How, for that matter, had it come to elect a hard-right Conservative government in 1983? What did this have to do with the way people talked to one another, and *were talked to*, about such matters? What did linguists, theorists of language, have to say about it all?

As it happened, 1984 reminded us all – sometimes *ad nauseam* – that George Orwell (no linguist, but an astute if wayward commentator on the political uses of language) had a great deal to say. The first chapter of this book takes a long view both of Orwell's contribution and of the way 'language' itself has been mythologised and mystified. Orwell's notion of language as an instrument of political control is examined further, in relation to more recent speculations in linguistics, in the two following chapters. Chapter 4 is an interlude that one might term 'semi-faction'. Its aim is to propose a critical, Orwell-inspired approach to the everyday language and communications media of our day. Chapter 5 applies such an approach to the verbal messages we all received at the time of the conflict between Britain and Argentina over the Falkland (or Malvinas) Islands. Chapter 6 takes a look at the most dangerous neo-Newspeak of all: 'nukespeak'. And, finally, Chapter 7 returns to linguistics and picks up a thread that runs through all the preceding chapters: metaphor – not as a poetic ornament, but as an everyday means of verbally constructing reality. What is provided in that chapter – and I hope in the rest of the book – is a toolkit, not just for the description of the verbal edifices which we daily inhabit, but for their dismantling and rebuilding.

Chapter 1 derives from a paper given at the sixth annual J. Lloyd Eaton conference on science fiction, July 1984. Chapter 2 is a version of a paper read at the *colloque* 'Orwell et la question du langage' organised by the International Sociological Association in Paris, November 1984. Chapters 3 and 4 are a version of Chapter 4 in P. Chilton & C. Aubrey (eds.), *Nineteen Eighty-Four in 1984* (Comedia, London, 1985). Chapter 6 first appeared, in an earlier form, in *Category B*, No. 4, March 1983 (Magill, South Australia). Chapter 8 derives in part from a talk given at the Institute of Contemporary Arts, August 6 (Hiroshima Day) 1981, and in part from a talk given to the Peace Pledge Union (I am not, incidentally, a pacifist in their sense) in October 1983. And Chapter 7 comes from an invited lecture to the Department of Behavioural and Communication Studies, the Polytechnic of Wales, February 1985. Chapter 9 originated as a talk to the Linguistics Circle at the University of Lancaster in November 1985. My thanks are due to all those who have commented on these papers and discussions.

Paul Chilton,
Coventry, 1988

1

Babel, Utopia and

Science Fictions of

Language

This chapter is about the relationship between a particular science, or would-be science, and certain works of fiction that also have as a major part of their purpose to project an alternative ideal form of social existence and/or to criticise an existing one. In so far as linguistics, science fiction and utopian narrative are separate sets,[1] I am interested in the intersection of those three sets. And in so far as they *do* intersect, I want to suggest that the distinctions between them can be usefully dismantled from time to time, in order to get a different insight into the way our culture thinks. That is the first introductory point.

The second point is best illustrated by the world's first experiment in linguistic science, recorded by Herodotus in the fifth century B.C. According to this well-known account, the Egyptian Pharaoh Psammetichus isolated two infants from human language in order to discover the natural, and therefore it was supposed the original, language of mankind. The experiment was replicated in the thirteenth century by the ruthless millenarian emperor Frederick II of Hohenstauffen, whose experimental subjects died, and by James IV of Scotland in the early sixteenth century, who discovered that *his* subjects acquired very good Hebrew, thus confirming the prevalent theological opinion on the matter. The continuation of this tale reveals even more clearly not only the role of the myth of the original human language, but also the role of political ideology in the science of language. A German scholar, J.G. Becanus, argued in the early seventeenth century that German must have been the primeval language spoken by Adam and Eve, since that language must have been a perfect language, and German *was* a perfect language. This was so, claimed Becanus, because the Germans had not contributed to the construction of the Tower of Babel, and so their tongue had not degenerated under the Curse of the Confusion. It would be wrong to think that rationalisations of this nature died out with the early days of Renaissance science. It is in fact my point that linguistic science, or at least that part of it selected for utilisation in imaginative literature, remains preoccupied with the quasi-mythical theme of the ideal and universal language well into Orwell's day and beyond, and that particular linguistic theories can be interpreted as reflecting philosophical, ethical and political concerns characteristic of their time.

To put things at their most general, what I want to suggest is that not only do certain linguistic theories possess the quality of fictions or myth, but also that the science fiction and utopian genres, when they make use of linguistic science (and no doubt the other sciences, too), do so in such a way as to imbue their symbolic stories with their own social significance. There is, I think, a striking continuity in the kind of linguistic theories or myths or obsessions that are taken up in such literature – so much so that it is quite easy to envisage examinations of the future asking silly questions like: what does Ian Watson have in common with Frederick II of Hohenstauffen? To which the not too silly, I hope, answer might be that both of them (Watson in *The Embedding*) tell tales of scientific experiments on language acquisition designed to probe the nature of human language, and that Watson binds this theme in with a set of political preoccupations characteristic of the late 1960s and early 1970s. Between Frederick and Watson there are others, not the least of whom is Orwell, and it is in this context that I think we might fruitfully set his notion of Newspeak in *Nineteen Eighty-Four*.

At the core of this continuity lies, as I've hinted, the story of the Tower of Babel. Its details and its presence in literature and linguistic speculation are well known from George Steiner;[2] but since there is still something to be said about its presence in science fiction and utopian literature, it is worth restating it in the relevant terms. As far as linguistic themes in these genres are concerned, the key motifs are (1) the idea of a lost language universal to all human beings, and (2) the idea that this lost language is 'natural', in the sense that its elements and structure correspond one to one with the elements and structures of reality. After God destroyed the Tower of Babel, language was confused, in the double sense that languages became mutually unintelligible, and that they no longer lucidly expressed the nature of things, but rather obscured and distorted them. The corollaries are important. One says that each post-Babel language is a closed system containing its own untranslatable view of the world. The second says that from the confusions and distortions of language stem misunderstandings, deception, social division and conflict.

It is these corollaries that have particular thematic prominence in the dystopias and science fiction of the twentieth century,[3] but there are other features of the basic Babel story that are also relevant to those genres, especially science fiction. The first is the theme of the technologically advanced society that over-reaches itself – the Tower, after all, is built to probe the skies. The second is the image of the Tower as a hierarchical, unified, total society. There is a third important element, which is of great importance in the post-Renaissance world and which one may or may not choose to link with the last two. It arises with the mechanisation of communication that makes its appearance with the development of the printing press, but also in connection with the desire of the philosophers of the seventeenth century to lay the curse of Babel by creating a universal language informed by the principles of mathematical and logical rigour. This is a line of thought that takes us away from the central Babel story and leads to the late twentieth-century problem of nature of machine intelligence and its science fiction reflexion in the shape of the tragi-comic computer, HAL.

With this nexus of themes in mind we can now try to trace their various manifestations from the classic Renaissance utopias in the sixteenth and seventeenth centuries, a period which saw the emergence of nation states, the standardisation of national languages, the discovery of cultures alien in both space and time, as well as explosion in actual travel, and in the diffusion of information via the new printing presses. It is scarcely surprising, therefore, to find what might be termed a 'Babelisation' of consciousness[4] – that is, renewed references to the Babel myth, a heightened sense of the relativity of separate languages, a desire to achieve universal communication, and at the same time a desire to achieve a harmonious golden-age community. At a time of rapid social change, More's unified, uniform communist *Utopia* represents order and stasis, with solid roots in the humanist's vision of antiquity. The specimen of Utopian language that More gives us in some respects symbolises the same themes. It is concocted out of Greek, Latin and perhaps Persian bits and pieces: the Utopians pick up Greek quickly, More tells us, and have a natural affinity with Greek literature and philosophy. The grammatical structure (specifically, the morphology) of the Utopian specimen is also partly reminiscent of the classical languages; but there are some features that are typical of the ideal, artificial, universal languages that literature and philosophy were to devise up in the following centuries. In particular, there is a simplification of vocabulary – a notable feature, you will remember, of Newspeak – achieved by combining basic elements which have fixed meanings, making the meaning of the resulting composite word transparent, rather in the way that in Newspeak the opposite of *good* is not *bad* but *ungood*. (The specimen of Utopian gives us *voluala* = *libenter* ('willingly'), *la volvola* = *gravatim* ('not willingly') and *la lavolvola* = *non gravatim* ('not not willingly'.)

Although Bacon's *New Atlantis* does not concern itself extensively with language, or offer us any imaginary utopian tongue, it is a crucial piece in the jigsaw, since it represents the interdependency of the main strands of the Babel paradigm – technology and knowledge, social order, and communication. Already in the *Novum Organum* (1620) and *The Advancement of Learning* (1605) Bacon had dwelt at length on the confused and misleading nature of languages. In the *Advancement* he actually evokes the mythical catastrophe of Babel, and suggests that the return to the state of grace will be accomplished through the science of grammar, as well as through the other sciences:

> For man still striveth to reintegrate himself in those benedictions from which by his fault he hath been deprived; and as he hath striven against the first general curse by the invention of all other arts, so hath he sought to come forth of the second general curse (which was the confusion of tongues) by the art of grammar...(XVI.4)

It is this task that is represented in the *New Atlantis*, where the ideal society is a new Babel – hierarchical, technocratic and aggressive. Significantly, the foundation myth that the narrative provides constitutes a laying of the Babel curse in a neo-pentecostal miracle: the people of Atlantis receive a Book which everyone, whatever their native language, can understand. The generation after Bacon was to propose blueprints, sometimes inspired by Chinese ideograms, for precisely such universal communication. Significantly, too, the New Atlantis includes amongst its technological advances long-distance communication systems and language machines of various kinds, all of which depend on the quest of information traders: there are knowledge missions to foreign parts every two years which sound uncannily like the deep space knowledge merchants of Ian Watson's *Embedding*. This is not the only link with subsequent fiction, for lurking behind Bacon's fantasy is a conception of science and language of historic social significance – a conception of science as the possession of a technocratic elite charged with the control, mastery and exploitation of nature or, as Bacon's metaphors revealingly put it, with 'the enlarging of the bounds of Human Empire':

> The End of our Foundation is the knowledge of Causes, and secret motions of thing; and the enlarging of the bounds of Human Empire, to the effecting of all things possible.

It seems, too, that closely bound up with this controlling, conquering conception of science – and it is, as Brian Easlea has argued, an essentially masculine conception – is the notion of supremacy in military technology. For while Bacon's Atlantans say that their scientific college, which is the pinnacle of their hierarchical social tower, is dedicated to social usefulness, it appears that part of this social utility is assumed to be victory in military competition:

> We have also engine houses...engines and instruments for all sorts of motions...we imitate and practise to make swifter motions than any you have...and to make them and multiply them more easily, and with smaller force, by wheels and other means; and to make them stronger, and more violent than yours are; exceeding your greatest cannons and basilisks. We represent also ordnance and instruments of war, and engines of all kinds: and likewise new mixtures and compositions of gun-powder, wild fires burning in water, and unquenchable...[5]

Bacon's call for an artificial language that would be universal and at the same time so structurally congruent with the universe that it would provide an instrument of all conceivable knowledge was abundantly answered in the seventeenth and eighteenth centuries. The titles are revealing and take us in an almost unbroken line to the linguistics, both scientific and fictional, of the twentieth century. In 1633 there was Comenius' *The Gate of Tongues Unlocked and Opened (Janua linguarum reserata e aperta)*, and in 1658 his *Visible World, or a Picture and Nomenclature of all the Chief Things That Are in the World*. Sir Thomas Urquhart's *Logopandecteision* (1653) is a mathematically based combinatorial system intended 'to appropriate the words of the universal language with the things of the universe.' The Reverend Cave Beck's *Universal Character* (1657) used the idea of Chinese ideograms for universal communication.

Nathaniel Smart neatly brought out both the mythic and socioeconomic basis of such attempts, calling Beck's system 'Babel reversed', and expressing the hope

> That divers languages no longer may
> Upon our trading such Embargoes lay.[6]

Dalgarno's *Ars Signorum, vulgo Character Universalis et Lingua Philosophica* (1668) received royal patronage. In the work of Leibniz there is a deep conviction that languages are closed (monadistic) systems determining thought and structuring experience, and at the same time a longing for a new universal language that would be based on mathematical and ideogrammatic principles and instantly legible by anyone.

But the most famous and influential of such thinkers was Bishop John Wilkins, who, besides his treatise on the possibility of life on the moon, offered to the Royal Society in 1661 an extraordinary *Essay Towards a Real Character and a Philosophical Language*. In deploring the deceptive and distorting natural of existing language Wilkins refers to 'the judgement inflicted on mankind in the Curse of the Confusion' at Babel. His system will redeem that mythical linguistic disaster

> by unmasking wild errors that shelter themselves under the disguise of affected phrases; which being philosophically unfolded, and rendered according to the genuine and natural importance of Words, will appear to be inconsistencies and contradictions. And several of those pretended, mysterious, profound notions, expressed in great swelling words, whereby some men set up for reputation, being this way examined, will appear to be, either nonsense, or very flat and jejune.

Human language is thus inherently debased, although it is typical of the ambivalence of this type of reasoning that 'men' can be also blamed for what they do with it. Since, however, language itself is seen as the prime culprit, it is nothing less than the whole human language system that has to be redeemed, that is, replaced by a rational 'Real Character' which, it is supposed, will not disguise or distort the true nature of things as they are. Wilkins's linguistic redemption, then, is to be accomplished in two theoretical steps.

The first is the tabulation into a classificatory system.[7] of all 'Things' and all 'Notions', which, as a rationalist, he believes to be *a priori* knowledge common to all men. The second is a 'reduction' of the vocabulary to a one-to-one correspondence with things and notions in a system of invariant base forms and addictive particles, plus the regularisation of grammatical rules. The first step is crucial, and the different philosophical view one can take of it accounts for the *dystopian* languages that arise in Swift and others, notably of course in Orwell. For example, Wilkins provides, amongst his other classifications of objective reality, a classification of social categories and their attributes. It is only necessary to read this in terms of *Nineteen Eighty-Four's* 'collective solipsism' instead of Wilkins's rationalism to arrive at the idea of Newspeak and thought control.

The link with Orwell is not as far fetched as it might seem. The intermediary is of course Swift. In his essay 'Politics vs. Literature' Orwell interprets Swift's *Voyage to Laputa* as an attack 'on what would now be called totalitarianism,' and, what is more important, he interprets the school of languages satirised by Swift as representing 'one of the main aims of totalitarianism': 'not merely to make people think the right thoughts, but actually to make them less conscious'.[8] Swift probably had in mind Wilkins Dalgarno and the Royal Society, particularly in his satire on the equation of words with things.[9]

In the *Voyage to Laputa* (Chapter V) Gulliver visits a 'School of Languages', where language experts are engaged in 'improving' the language of their country, and in mechanising it ('a project for improving speculative Knowledge by practical and mechanical Operations'). It is worth quoting the passage in full, because in it Swift's sarcasm strongly links the mechanisation of language with a technocratic elite that is both dominated by men and opposed to (though, it appears, ultimately inhibited by) the wishes and interest of the people:

> The first Project was to shorten Discourse by cutting Polysyllables into one, and leaving out Verbs and Participles; because in Reality all things imaginable are but Nouns.
>
> The other was a scheme for abolishing all Words whatsoever: And this was urged as a great Advantage in Point of Health as well as Brevity. For it is plain, that every Word we speak is in some Degree a Diminution of our Lungs by Corrosion; and consequently contributes to the shortening of our Lives. An Expedient was therefore offered, that since Words are only names of *Things*, it would be more convenient for all Men to carry about them, such *Things* as were necessary to express the particular Business they are to discourse on. And this Invention would certainly have taken Place, to the great Ease as well as Health of the Subject, if the Women in Conjunction with the Vulgar and Illiterate had not threatened to raise a Rebellion, unless they be allowed the Liberty to speak with their Tongues, after the Manner of their Forefathers: Such constant irreconcilable Enemies to Science are the Common People. However, many of the most Learned and Wise adhere to the new Scheme of expressing themselves by *Things*...

Whether Orwell knew about Wilkins and the rest, the fact remains that the main linguistic points picked up by Swift – namely, the mechanisation of language, combinatorial systems, the 'reduction' of vocabulary and grammar, the fixing of meanings, and the equation of words with things – all these points are to found almost verbatim in the mouths of the Newspeak experts Syme and O'Brien. The crucial insight in both Swift and Orwell is that language can operate in the exercise of power – and not only language. In Swift's satire masculine Baconian science has taken over the domain of language in the academy. In *Nineteen Eighty-Four* language science has seized power.

This is not the whole linguistics context for *Nineteen Eighty-Four*. Nineteenth-century linguistics provided further contributory ideas and myths, the literary exploitation of which is best exemplified in Bulwer-Lytton's utopian prophecy *The Coming Race* (1871).

Nationalism in politics and evolutionism in biology are matched in linguistics by the development of comparative and historical methods. There are three prominent strands in this development. The first is the reversal of the confusion of Babel in the discovery that all the separate European and Indo-Iranian languages could be related to one another in a single family'. Sanskrit was the missing link which was systematically compared with Greek and Latin to establish a primal proto-language, designated Aryan by German scholars. The second strand is linguistic relativity, according to which language is not, as the rationalists saw it, a particularisation of a universal structure, but rather a mould for specific thought patterns. Herder is associated with this approach at the end of the eighteenth century, and more importantly Wilhelm von Humboldt, who spoke of language not as a direct correlate of the world, but as a third universe', hovering between the universe of phenomena and the inner universe of consciousness. Each culture, according to this view, has its own *innere Sprachform* which determines thought. Both the relativity and the determinism persist in the notorious Sapir-Whorf hypothesis, attributed to two ethno-linguists working in America in the early decades of the twentieth century, and according to which one's conception of 'the real world' is entirely a product of the structure of the language one happens to speak. The third, distinctly ideological, strand claimed that particular languages can be classified in a hierarchy of excellence with respect to the kind of word-structure they exhibit. At the top were the 'inflectional' languages like Sanskrit, Greek and Latin, in the middle the 'agglutinative' languages like Turkish which built their words out of segments with specific values, and at the bottom were 'isolating' languages like Chinese and the American Indian languages.

Now the link with Bulwer-Lytton is simple and explicit. The idea that the three morphological types correlated with three levels of social organisation and social excellence was put about by the populariser of linguistic science, Max Müller, and it is on Müller's ideas that Bulwer-Lytton bases his imaginary ideal language in *The Coming Race*. The symbolic use in the novel of these linguistic theories tend to confirm Raymond Williams's view that this utopia is essentially an aristocratic projection.[10] The society described by Bulwer-Lytton depends on the technology of a new energy source that he calls Vril, and which has removed the old modes of production and transformed social relations. Yet it has transformed them into a mirror image of the aristocratic world. Haunted by the spectre of the French and American revolutions, Bulwer-Lytton presents a coming race that displays the manners and refinements of the best noble families. In particular, the supposed sexual equality of the Vril utopia is an aristocratic inversion. The women are intelligent, seven feet tall and woo their own mates, and the word for them in the utopian language is, we are told, *Gy* after the Greek (but they are none the less really guys in disguise, and bound by the rules of an aristocratic patriarchy). The novel's tenuous narrative is in fact the traditional aristocratic one, hinging on the fear of fouling the blood of the race by a union with a being lower down the evolutionary ladder. The linguistics reflect the same outlook. The narrator tells us that the Vril-ya are 'originally... as seems... clear by the roots of their language, descended from the same ancestors as the great Aryan family, from which in varied streams has flowed the dominant civilisation of the world'.[11] Bulwer-Lytton's utopian language is both of the future and of the past. It expresses its primal nobility by the presence of those isolating morphemes which Müller claimed reflected the family stage of social development, and it expresses its advanced evolutionary stage by the (alleged) presence of flexional features which Müller claimed to be typical of politically advanced societies. Structures which are typical of the American Indian languages – 'polysynthetic monsters...devouring invaders of the aboriginal forms', as Lytton calls them – are ruthlessly rooted out.

There are here some pre-echoes of Orwell's notion of dystopian language: his dislike of composite words and 'prefabricated' phrases, which he too called 'barbarous'; his idea in *Nineteen Eighty-Four* of a language morphologically tailored to the culture of Ingsoc; and his idea of the ideologically motivated grammarians who plan its structure. But the idea of language as an evolving natural organism, which lay behind the reconstructive work of the Romantic philologists, was actually inimical to Orwell and explicitly rejected by him. For him language was rather 'an instrument which we shape for our own purposes',[12] and the dominant metaphor for him, as for much of twentieth-century linguistic speculation, is an engineering one – the structure, the system, the mechanisms that can be constructed, controlled and exploited.

The web of linguistic ideas in the air at the time Orwell was active is a complex one. But a clue to the relevant themes is provided by a fact pointed out only, so far as I know, by Brian Aldiss – that Orwell's dystopia was published within a year of the science fiction language fantasy *The World of Null-A* by A.E. Van Vogt.[13] These two books, despite their enormous differences, make use of the same pool of linguistic ideas – ideas which are in many respects a continuation of the tradition of Wilkins and Leibniz.

The turn of the nineteenth century had seen a spate of universal language schemes, whose declared aim was the easing of international communication, although the old rationalist desire to capture the pre-Babel natural truthfulness of language structure remains. There is J.-M. Schleyer's Volapük (which is Volapük for 'worldspeak') of 1879; Zamenhof's Esperanto of 1887, with its strict determinacy and regularity; G. Henderson's Latinesce of around 1900; the Interlingua of the mathematician Giuseppi Peano in 1903; Jespersen's Novial; and several others up to Hogben's Interglossa of 1943, which was known to Orwell, and half admired, half mocked by him.[14] C.K. Ogden's *Basic English* (1930) is also designed as a universal language. Behind the choice of English lies an inversion of Müller and Bulwer-Lytton's notion of the evolution of structural types: Ogden argues that English has evolved towards structural simplicity and semantic purity, and is thus truly '*basic* for the whole world'.[15] It is also seen as basic in the sense that, like the schemes of Bishop Wilkins and the rest, it claims to represent true facts of nature, for 'the fundamental operations of physics ... when caused by the human organism as a whole can be covered ... by ten of the sixteen operational symbols in the Basic vocabulary'.[16]

All this, and much more about Basic, would have been well known to Orwell, who corresponded with Ogden, was from time to time favourably disposed towards an international language, and apparently considered promoting Basic at the BBC and through *Tribune*.[17] But it is quite plausible to read the Newspeak sections of *Nineteen Eighty-Four* as satirical parody of the Babel-breaking Basic, much as Swift satirised *The Real Character*. Perhaps it was a certain authoritarian, even imperialistic, streak in Ogden's little book that turned utopian Basic into the dystopian Newspeak for Orwell. At any rate the parody is unmistakeable. Ogden deplores the remaining inflectional irregularities of English that 'mar the grammatical picture', as do the Newspeak grammarians. The reduction of vocabulary, and especially of verbs, is the guiding principle. 'Verbs involve a wasteful vocabulary,' says Ogden.[18] 'The great wastage is in the verbs,' echoes Syme.[19] Ogden recommends that all antonyms should be formed regularly and transparently: for example, *straight/unstraight*, etc.[20] And Syme: 'What need is there for a word like "bad"? "Ungood" will do just as well...' With Syme, Ogden might well have said, 'It's a beautiful thing, the destruction of words.'

It needs to be added that this particular kind of quest for an ideal universal language is not unconnected with the more rigorously scientific quest of Russell and Whitehead, with its roots in the logic of Boole, Peano and Frege, and its diverse continuations in Wittgenstein, the Logical Positivists of the 1930s, and perhaps the formally explicit computer languages of today. What has Orwell to do with all this? There is a personal link through Ogden (the translator and editor of Wittgenstein) and through A.J. Ayer.[21] It is difficult to imagine Orwell poring over the *Tractatus*, but there are none the less some suggestive parallels. Wittgenstein's work, regarded by Russell at least as an attempt at an ideal language, 'a logically perfect language',[22] presented a closed system which literally *pictures* an exactly corresponding reality, a system that permitted the valid inference of true propositions concerning that reality, a system that can say nothing of reality outside itself and nothing about itself. Consider now what this might mean when translated into the kind of political terms that interested Orwell as a writer. Instead of Wittgenstein, read Winston and Syme. It would mean a system designed to refer to an objective reality, but to a desired and prescribed one. The Newspeak of the Ingsoc language planners is such a system: it corresponds term by term with a certain political reality, it is supposed to permit only ideologically 'true' inferences, and it is supposed to render inaccessible other realities and to make criticism of itself impossible.

Orwell had already touched on some of these matters in his significantly titled and little read essay 'New Words'. The first striking thing about that essay is the use of mathematical and mechanical metaphors. Language is conceived as a post-Babel nightmare of distortion and falsification, against which Orwell dreams of a language in which 'expressing one's meaning [would be] a matter of taking the right words and putting them in place, like working out an equation in algebra.'[23] Second, the motive for this dream is presented as a desire to make language directly express personal experience of the world, for Orwell thinks of language primarily as a vehicle of thought. He seems to envisage some rational group of people collectively able, in some unspecified way, 'to *show* meaning in some unmistakeable form', and then, in a second stage, giving this meaning a name. 'The question is simply of finding a way in which one can give thought an objective existence,' we are told.[24] This two-stage process sounds uncannily like the two-tier edifice of 'collective solipsism' (deciding on approved meanings) and the vocabulary of Newspeak (giving names to those meanings) that we have in *Nineteen Eighty-Four*. And, thirdly, this dream of a perfect language leads to a language myth that properly belongs with Plato's linguistic naturalism. 'It seems probable,' declares Orwell, 'that a word, even a not yet existing word, has as it were a natural form,' by which he means 'a correlation between the sound of a word and its meaning',[25] so that language appears no longer as an arbitrary and indirect code, but as a direct picture of meaning. New Words and Newspeak are the utopian and dystopian sides of the same coin. One of the functions of the novel *Nineteen Eighty-Four* is to investigate fictionally what happens when the utopian language myth is set in a social and political context. It is an interesting coincidence that the linguist who best understood these matters, J.R. Firth, had written in 1937: 'World languages are made not by amateur grammarians but by world powers...They are built on blood, money, sinews, and suffering in the pursuit of power.'[26]

Van Vogt's *The World of Null-A* relates to the ideal language myth in a simpler and completely uncritical way. 'Null-A' is the allegedly non-Aristotelian system of Alfred Korzybski, to whom the novel is dedicated: he had founded an Institute of General Semantics to promote the ideas contained in his book *Science and Sanity* (1933). Many of the component ideas, such as the mystificatory misuse of language, the dangers of abstract words, of emotionally loaded terms, of illicit dichotomies, etc., are to be found in Orwell, but the whole orientation of his theory is the reverse of what appears to be Orwell's final position. Korzybski claimed to be doing for language what Riemann and Lobatchevski had done for mathematics, and what Einstein had done for physics. Although he stopped short of his predecessors in the ideal language tradition in declining to devise an artificial language or revise an existing one in the way Ogden had done, he did make far-reaching claims for his proposed modification of what he called the semantic structure of language. This, in effect, meant adjusting the mental habits in the use of language which he believed to be the result of centuries of education by men trained in Aristotelian logic. The dangers of the traditional Aristotelian mode of thought lay in the use of two-valued logic, which led to statements like 'X is either right or wrong.' His own system was supposed, by contrast, to reflect modern multi-valued logics, which would lead to statements like 'X may be a bit right and/or a bit wrong.' He reduced this to Aristotle's 'law of identity', which he regarded as misleading in all spheres of application. For instance, Smith is not the same Smith in 1930 as he was in 1920. This line of thought was to give Van Vogt the central idea for his novel. What is not clear in Korzybski is where 'mental orientation' stops and language starts: there is a tendency to attribute the universal confusion which he seeks to redeem to the structure of language itself. Accordingly, in the tradition of the Babel myth, he believed that 'Any map or language ... should, in structure, be similar to the structure of the empirical world. Likewise, from the point of view of a theory of sanity, any system or language should, in structure, be similar to the structure of our nervous system.'[27] Since that homology did not exist, 'unsanity' or confusion and conflict was normal in human affairs, but was due to be remedied by the inauguration of a new era, of which he regarded himself the prophet. Where Korzybski, and with him Van Vogt, differ from Orwell is in their view of the relationship between language and political power. Although Korzybski is often reminiscent of Orwell in his criticism of the propaganda use of language, he seems to adopt the view that language (that is, the old unredeemed language) is actually the *cause* of the abuse of political power, and in particular of Nazism. Orwell is careful with respect to this question of causality, and makes clear that he thinks that 'the decline of a language must ultimately have political and economic causes'.[28] In Korzybski's belief, on the other hand, it would seem to follow that the adoption of the null-A language will usher in a universal utopia.

This is indeed more or less the underlying thesis of Van Vogt's *World of Null-A*. The seeming confusion of the story, which has dismayed critics, [29] is no more than a transposition into narrative conventions of Korzybski's notion of non-identity, and his generalised view of the universe as a dynamic process characterised by unpredictable quantum leaps. So the hero Gosseyn (Go-sane) has three bodies, two brains and is frequently displaced without warning from one location in the solar system to another. Similar things happen to the subsidiary characters, whose identities and roles are sometimes made ambiguous, sometimes reversed – no doubt to tease the two-valued Aristotelian reader whose reading conventions lead him to expect his goodies and baddies to be drawn in black and white. In principle this game is not dissimilar to the surprise effects Orwell works into *Nineteen Eighty-Four* through the characters of O'Brien and Mr Charrington. But beyond the narrative there are rather simple thematic patterns. The first is mythic and religious, and draws out the similar elements in Korzybski's supposedly scientific work. The capital city of Van Vogt's null-A society has at its centre a Tower housing a gigantic machine programmed with artificial intelligence and speech synthesis and recognition capacities. This symbol of a renewed Babel is what one might expect from the tradition I have outlined. The tower is the temple of null-A, which, we are told, has its 'sacred symbols' and its 'converts'. Gosseyn himself is presented, with his one-in-three, three-in-one identity, as a 'saviour', a sacrificial victim, controlled by a 'cosmic chess player' with whom he turns out to be identical, and for whose sake he, by implication, rescues null-A. The second pattern reflects a view of contemporary international politics, although geography has become galactic. A perfect null-A utopia exists on Venus, but on Earth the competitive selection by examination of the best null-A brains is liable to be undermined by corrupt politicians in league with the forces of non-null-A, that is a Galactic Empire which is aggressive, militaristic, expansionist, and of course the deadly foe of null-A ideology and peace. In between, the Galactic League, which ineffectively tries to keep Galactic peace, is a thinly disguised projection of the League of Nations as Korzybski portrayed it in its ideal form in *Science and Sanity* – that is, committed to the ideology of null-A rather than to any other.[30] The interesting thing about *World of Null-A* is that in its fundamental structure it represents just the two-valued schema, perhaps even the 'primitive' patterns, that it claims to be replacing.

In the post-war period the rapid explosion in electronic communications was accompanied by a no less bewildering proliferation of radically new departures in linguistic science, though the work of Chomsky at least has acknowledged roots in the rationalism and universalism of the seventeenth century. It is not surprising to find post-war science fiction that revives the Babel myth, and does so by using the new linguistics in a symbolic fashion.

Clarke's *2001* uses the work of the 1970s in speech synthesis and recognition to symbolise not so much the inadequacies of computers as the fallen nature of man. Even the writing of science fiction becomes experimental, reflecting structuralist themes, and symbolising social and political perspectives, as in the hybrid Russo-English jargon of Burgess' dystopian *Clockwork Orange* (1962), which is a straightforward enactment of the myth of post-Babel linguistic conflict. Samuel Delay's *Babel-17* (1967) utilises the structuralist conception of language, which encouraged the idea of the closed mechanical system, to develop utopian and dystopian themes. Yet there is also a shadowy political pattern to the plot, common enough in popular science fiction – namely, the frustration of the plans of an evil invader. The heroine of *Babel-17* is a linguist who succeeds in decoding the language of an alien power and defusing its ultimate weapon – the implantation in the minds of its victims of a sinister incapacitating language system. The mythic elements abound. Our heroine is confronted with the post-Babel confusion of tongues on a galactic scale. 'Babel-17', however, the language of the evil invader, is an ideal language conforming to traditional conceptions: we are told that it is concise, precise, harmonious, and contains its pure meanings by virtue of a natural relationship between the signifying word and the thing signified. But it turns out to be also an artificial language, an invention of the aliens, whose base design is a language transplant. Specifically, the all-important pronouns *I* and *you* have been excluded from this language. The consequence of this exclusion, according to the novel and in accordance with the rigid interpretation of the Whorf theory that one's language utterly determines one's possible thoughts, is that humans will no longer be capable of knowing the distinction between self and other, self and alien, and will become subservient machines. (Yet how, one wonders, would the invaders prevent people reinventing the pronouns, or any other words? This is also the problem for Orwell's Newspeak linguists.) In this novel, there is a clear line from the Babel myth, through ideal language fantasies, to the Orwellian dystopia and the political nightmares of our time. It is extraordinary that language is imagined to play so large a part in these fantasies of doom and oppression, and that the world, nay the universe, is saved by a linguist. In the beginning was the Word – and the divine linguist. All this might be of no consequence whatsoever, were it not that there appear to be people in political life who have similar fantasies: the notion of 'semantic infiltration' of western minds by the alien Soviets and their liberal agents, as we shall note in Chapter 9, is apparently taken seriously by some in the defence community.

There is a large corpus of other science fiction texts in which linguistic ideas play a greater or lesser part. But in tracing the linkage between linguistic myths and political themes, one work of science fiction in particular is significant. Ian Watson's *Embedding* (1973) is not only a rich and final statement of the Babel myth, but also a political novel that links it in some ways to the Orwellian dystopia, though the dystopia has now filled the universe. As in Delany's novel, language is the threat, and linguists the heroes and villains. The explicit use of Chomsky's linguistics, and the less explicit use of Levi-Strauss's anthropology, are in fact little more than what Levi-Strauss himself called *bricolage* – the construction of a symbolic structure that enables you to think out of any available bric-a-brac. There would be theoretical difficulties if Watson's use of the notions of 'embedding' and 'universal grammar' were taken literally. 'Embedding' in Chomsky's linguistics refers to certain syntactic structures, and 'universal grammar' has to do with specifying the formal limitations on humanly learnable grammars. If you embed one sentence inside another inside another inside another…'recursively', that is, the claim is that all human brains will boggle. For example, *The book (the linguist wrote) is on the shelf* causes no processing problems. But try putting another sentence inside this one: *the book (the linguist [the critics loathed] wrote) is on the shelf*. Even worse: *the book (the linguist [the critic (the publishers paid) loathed] wrote) is on the shelf*. My point is that Chomsky's embedding is about grammatical structures, while Watson seems interested in thinkable thoughts, the boundaries and limitations of what humans can conceive. Watson's use of narratives embedded one within the other is aesthetically appealing, but the implicit appeal to science, in the form of Chomskyan linguistics, is erroneous. Really relevant ideas on language are those formulated in differing ways by the Whorf hypothesis and Wittgenstein's *Tractatus* – namely, that the limits of my language mean the limits of my universe. Even more generally, what we have in the novel looks more like a peculiarly rich restatement of the Babel themes – the lost primal language of the universe, which is attuned to ultimate reality, the confusion of tongues, cultural incomprehension and political deceit, and finally the total destruction that follows an attempt to recover the lost language. 'Embedding' means being trapped in conceptional relativity and individuality, as opposed to collectivity and communication.

It is thus used to weave a political statement that reflects the context of the 1970s – a statement that sometimes has more in common with Chomsky's politics of the 1960s than with his linguistics, but which has the bleakness of Orwell's *Nineteen Eighty-Four*.[31] Orwell's Airstrip I is now a U.K. in which research institutes have a devious military link-up; linguistic research, less directly but more plausibly, than Orwell's Newspeak, is embedded, as it were, in the apparatus of state security and social control. As in Van Vogt, there is a corrupt, militaristic and assertive 'empire', but this time it is the United States in collusion, it is hinted, with the Soviet Union. This is an 'empire', we are told, bent on extending its influence in the third world, and on deceiving its own population. There are explicit criticisms of official secrecy and the use of psychological techniques of manipulation. This is a post-Babel world in which language is used only to deceive, and in which the psycholinguist hero who tries to transcend human language only brings death and destruction. The novel offers no escape either in the 'primitive' universe of the noble savage, or in the advanced stage of evolution reached by the alien linguists from the stars. The 'embedded' language of the imaginary Amazonian tribe serves to symbolise a profoundly alien conception of reality, but also to symbolise a futile desire to control reality through language that is inseparable from the exercise of power. The chief initiate of the 'embedded' language emerges as no more – and no less – than 'a village Hitler'. The alien race from the stars is also in search of the missing language of transcendant reality – yet they too emerge as exploiting merchants prepared to trade in disembodied brains. In the universe of discourse set up by the novel the supposed impossibility of crossing the barriers of language or languages stands for the impossibility of leaving a moral and political universe. All attempts to do so lead to death or madness. The one thing that remains, and which in fact permits the denouement of the narrative, is the exercise of force in the shape of nuclear weapons, used to destroy the alien searchers after truth.

What conclusions can we draw from this fragmentary survey? Looking back from Watson to Bacon, one is struck by an evolution that is a *reversal*.

Bacon's island utopia has become a cosmic dystopia. Bacon's 'enlargement of the Human Empire' through science has found its absolute limits, and has become an empire, in the political sense, of scientific deception and destruction. The universal language of knowledge and truth has given way to conflict of codes and destructive delusions. Above all, the integration of science and society dreamed of by Bacon has turned out to be corrupt and oppressive. One cannot help feeling that the seeds of this reversal were present from the start in the conception of science – and of language, perhaps – which Bacon represented

2

Language, Nature,

Culture

How then, shall we conceive 'language'? On this question the whole project of the criticism of 'language' depends, for if 'language' is thought of in the particular way that it often is, then it is not immediately obvious that it makes sense to speak of criticising language at all. This is to say that there is an ambiguity in our use of the term 'language': in some senses of the term it seems to make sense, but not in others. What are these senses? An analogy may serve us here (although analogies can be slippery beasts, as we shall see below).

It seems to make little sense to speak of criticising rocks or trees – except, and here is the crucial clue, in so far as rocks or trees are being thought of as arranged (for aesthetic or utilitarian purposes, say) by some human, and it seems to be necessarily human, agency. That is, it is decidedly odd to say that one is being critical of some rocks, unless one conjures up a context in which rocks are an *objet d'art*, a rockery, a barricade, or some such. A plausible context depends on social institutions and roles of many kinds, and the ascription of intention to a human agent. In brief, rocks can be natural objects or they can be the instruments of human action. To criticise rocks in the former sense does not seem to mean a lot. It is quite meaningful, on the other hand, to criticise them in the latter sense. Analogously, one can consider what it might mean to criticise language conceived as either a natural phenomenon or a form of human action. What would it mean to criticise language in the first sense – that is, as a natural phenomenon, a given and unchangeable characteristic of the human species? The answer, it seems to me, is not a lot – no more than it does to criticise rocks in a similar sense. Unless, perhaps, one does so in some theological sense, in which it is sensible to criticise human nature (and thus human language) as fallen, degenerate, unredeemed, tainted by original sin, and so forth.

That way lies the verbal Fall from the Edenic language, Babel, logophobia and the desire for redemptive language schemes. What would it mean on the other hand to criticise language as the instrument of human action? It seems clear that this would be tantamount to criticising the action itself. To criticise language would mean to criticise human actions, that is, evaluate them with respect to some frame of values, which would, to say no more than the bare minimum, involve beliefs about truth, freedom and justice. In broad terms I take it that an *Orwellian linguistics* will be a *critical linguistics*, or *critical theory of language*, which steers a course (not always a steady course in Orwell's own case, as we have seen in Chapter 1) between the Scylla of narrow linguistic prescriptivism (thou shalt not split infinitives) and the Charybdis of a generalised logophobia that blames all ills on 'language' itself.

This knot concerning the meaning of language is only beginning to be unravelled, even by linguists. It is Orwell who, in his undoubtedly confused way, should alert us in the 1980s to the way in which so-called linguistic sciences can be permeated by misleading or even damaging models, metaphors and analogies, as well as to the ways in which language-as-social-practice can be misleading and even damaging. We need, then, in the first instance to look at the ways in which the Laputan professors have represented to themselves the object of their study, and to situate in that context the Orwellian project for a critique of 'language'.

While language study in the shape of ancient rhetoric conceived itself as a *political science*, modern linguistics has represented itself as a *natural science*. Natural sciences come, of course, in various forms. Nineteenth-century historical philology thought in terms of evolutionary biology, and frequently represented language as an autonomous organism, *a natural growth* – a model or metaphor which Orwell himself noticed and rejected at the beginning of his essay on 'Politics and the English Language'. Now the choice of metaphor is not just an aesthetic matter – because any metaphorical model contains the potential for inferences which can be transferred back to the object of study.[1] In the case of the natural growth metaphor, it follows, for example that the scope for controlling language (or the right to do so) is restricted. This is why Orwell uses metaphors from engineering and construction instead: language is 'an instrument we can shape for our own purposes'.[2] He also however, especially in the essay 'New Words' (a foreshadowing, perhaps, of Newspeak), uses metaphors from mathematics and logic – metaphors which are fundamental, of course, to the early Wittgenstein and the logical positivists, but also, I would suggest, to Saussure with his notion of language as a system of pure relations.[3] At any rate, there is a certain ambivalence in Orwell which is highly indicative of the kind of problem we are up against in seeking to define a critical theory of language. On the one hand, he has this almost utopian notion of a totally determinate language where each linguistic item corresponds to each thought with mathematical necessity and perspicuity. Perhaps linked with this desire for determinacy in Orwell is a streak of mechanistic determinism: the decline of a language, he asserts in 'Politics and the English Language', must ultimately have political and economic causes. That 'must' and that 'ultimately' beg, of course, the very questions we need to investigate. On the other hand, there is a marked tendency towards what some commentators have called his 'voluntarism'.[4] This 'voluntarism' can be interpreted in two senses. In its primary sense, it refers to the supposed ability of the individual conscious subject to determine the expression of his already conceived meaning by using language as a given resource. In another sense, it can be referred to Orwell's notion that the resource itself – language – is not a natural resource, but is itself constructed, as in his grotesque language engineering experiment, Newspeak. There is an important difference between the first and the second senses: the first is associated with the individual's struggle with the indeterminacies of the language resource, and with a (somewhat Romantic) idea of creativity; the second implies the reverse – structural and semantic determinacy, the bounded nature of language, and thus the absence of creativity and change.

There is a curious potential link here between these two notions of Orwellian 'voluntarism', as Carl Freedman argues. If you hold, as Orwell often did, that the individual conscious subject can by an effort of the will control the language, you may end up with the notion that a collection of individuals, by means of some form of political power, can control 'language' in the way the Newspeak grammarians do in *Nineteen Eighty-Four*. This *unconstrained* linguistic 'voluntarism' starts with the notion that the individual speaker is a free subject, that 'language' is an unbounded external resource, that thought determines language. And it ends up with the reverse – the linguistic determination of thoughts. Let's call this the 'Orwellian paradox' – a bit unfairly, since it is only implicit in what he says – which pinpoints the central problematic for a critical linguistics.

Another way of stating the problem is in terms of the nature/culture dichotomy – an ideological distinction, to be sure, but one that is amenable to rational elucidation. The 'Orwellian paradox' arises precisely because that distinction is not made, or the problem not posed. The question is one which, as I see it, theoretical linguistics, psycholinguistics and sociolinguistics need to approach jointly. Essentially, Orwell forces upon us the following question: Which part or parts of the phenomena we call 'language' or 'a language', fall within the category 'nature', which in the category 'culture'? To state the problem in those terms is to ask more detailed questions such as: Which parts of 'language' *can* be regarded as socially determined objects? Which are a-social components of human nature? Which parts of 'language' can be consciously known and in such cases controlled? Which are inaccessible to consciousness? What Orwell on language does, I think, is lead us to fix the terms in some such way, so that we can ask what we mean by 'language' or 'a language'; and it is in this sense that we might put forward theoretical suggestions concerning Saussure and Chomsky and their implications for a critical linguistics.

The Saussurean model of language is one that tends to privilege a bounded and determinate conception of language; at the same time, it can be seen as expressing a social theory. The significant thing is the way Saussure manipulates his initial tripartite schema of *langue* (a language), *parole* (individual speech) and *langage* (the human language faculty as a whole). Of these three categories it is perhaps *langage* that we might find to be the most useful focus for the critical questions we have posed: namely, how far is human language natural, universal, conscious, controllable, and so on? And, as a matter of fact, Saussure *does* at one point broach the the naturalness question on the physiological level; but he does so only in order to assert that 'ce n'est pas le langage qui est naturel à l'homme mais la faculte *de constituer une langue*' ('it is not the spoken language that is nature to man but the faculty of constituting a language') (p. 26). The trouble here seems to be the word *constituer*, which has strong socio-political implications; if that is so, the tendency of the sentence is to naturalise the social and, effectively, to evade investigation of the social and political processes by means of which one language variety can get promoted to the status of *une langue* ('a language'). A similar effect is, of course, achieved by the methodological prescription of synchrony (the study of *une langue* frozen at a point in time) and the exclusion of diachrony (the study of *une langue* through time). What happens in approaches of this kind is that the idea of 'a language' becomes reified – established as if it were a natural, objective entity independent of human agencies. If Saussurean linguistics falls into this position, it does so under the influence of Durkheim's notion of the objectively given 'social fact' made up of a system of rules and norms. While this conception avoids the extreme view that there is nothing real in society but the individual, it contains within it an implied legitimation of a particular social system.[5] What it means as far as linguistic theory is concerned is that *langage*, language, the total capacity of humans for communication, gets neglected, and whatever theoretical insights Saussure formulated (such as the concept of paradigmatic and syntagmatic relations) get attributed to a social-cultural entity (*une langue*, 'a language') rather than to natural abilities. This problem is compounded, be it noted in passing, for English speakers because of the potential confusion of the expressions *language* and *a language*.[6]

Three further points should suggest a strange parallel between the Saussurean *langue* myth and the Orwellian Newspeak parable. First, Saussure's text strongly suggests that the notion of *langage* is governed by a *language-as-nature* metaphor, *langue* by a mechanistic (or perhaps mathematical) one. We are told for example that *langage* is 'multiforme' and 'heteroclite' while *langue* is 'un tout en soi', a bounded system of interacting components. While nature and culture remain locked in these categories, the possibility of investigating their respective scopes is reduced. They are also the very categories – the unbounded and indeterminate as opposed to the bounded and determinate – that occur in Orwell's reflexions on language. Second, the account Saussure gives of *la langue* in relation to *la parole* can be read metaphorically as a social theory, whose main elements are the concept of order ('la langue est ... un principe de classification' [p. 25] etc.), the myth of the social contract ('elle n'éxiste qu'en vertu d'une sorte de contrat passé entre les membres de la communauté'), and, most important, the belief that the social order is a Durkheimian 'objective fact' which coerces individuals because it is located in their minds, shapes their thoughts, constitutes them as speaking subjects, and indeed constitutes reality by imposing form on the amorphous mush of experience. Now most of this, it seems to me, is consistent with the theory of language implicit in Orwell's satirical appendix on Newspeak; but the specific difference is crucial. Orwell's exaggerated fable gives us not the harmonious myth of the tacit social contract, or the notion of convention; rather, he explicitly introduces the concept of power into the historical process of language promotion and planning. That is not say that he resolves the question as to how far the social control of language is possible, but to have posed the question is something.

My general point is that the Saussurean model is not calculated to provide a toe-hold for a critical linguistics. Nor, one might think, is the Chomskyan mentalist model, especially in view of the fact that the Chomskyan categories of *competence* and *performance* are often linked up with *langue* and *parole*.[7] However, it is arguable, and has been argued in an important article by Trevor Pateman,[8] that Chomsky's model *is*, paradoxical as it may seem, quite compatible with a sociolinguistics, including a critical sociolinguistics. This is so because of the claims made by its mentalism (its concern with language as an organ of the *mind*) and because the nativist idea that language ability is an inborn and therefore universal human endowment raises precisely the question of how far and in what sense the phenomenon we call 'language' is (a) amenable to conscious control and construction, and (b) subject to social determination. Pateman's argument, put broadly, is that Chomskyan nativism (the view that language is an innate universal organ specific to *Homo sapiens*) does not have to be developed exclusively as a 'naturalist' theory, but can provide a theoretical model for understanding the interaction of nature *and* culture.

It will suffice for present purposes to draw out some significant points of difference between Saussure's *langue* on the one hand and Chomsky's concept of *competence* on the other. First, competence is conceived not as a social construct, but as knowledge of a grammar of a language whose constraints are the principles of universal innate grammar. We are clearly in the domain of the *natural*, for it makes sense within this Chomskyan nativist model to speak, as Pateman does, of language *growth*, and even of a grammar growing within the individual subject. The latter phrase indicates that we are dealing with a concept quite different from the strictly phylogenetic 'language-as-natural organism' metaphor that Orwell disliked. This does not exclude, however, the view that social interaction both triggers and shapes the growth. Second, unlike Saussure's *langue*, Chomsky's competence emphasises (a) the individual and (b) creativity – creativity in the sense of tacit knowledge capable of generating an infinite set of novel sentences. Competence thus straddles *langue* and *parole* and contains some of the free creativity hinted at in parts of Orwell.

Thirdly, competence in the specific sense of a mentally represented grammar is but a part of the total communicative competence of the subject. The nativist claim is in fact that grammars are *nsufficient* as explanations of speech and understanding: much more is required, including cultural norms and practices of various kinds. This distinction is an important one, because some theorists of literature and culture, for instance Jonathan Culler, have equivocated on the term competence in a way that equates culture and social practices with grammar, and thus naturalises these practices in a way that reduces the possibility of critique.[9] It implies for instance that verbal deception or distortion is attributed not to individual agents or to social practices but to language as a reified entity. This is one form of *logophobia*.

If, however, we recognise Chomskyan competence as a subpart of general communicative ability, I think the nativist framework (which Pateman incidentally characterises as yielding an anarchist social theory) does open the way for a critical linguistics.[10] It does so, first, because the notion of the growth of grammar explicitly raises questions concerning which components of a grammar are *natural* and *asocial* and which are *cultural forms*. Syntactic structures such as Subject-Verb-Object word order, the reliance of rules on grammatical categories, do not seem to be inherently cultural or ideological; on the other hand, the structure of the lexicon can plausibly be seen as culturally formed, though how far remains to be investigated. The second thing about the nativist view of competence is that it leaves open the rest of communicative competence for the development of critical theories of communication.

It leaves the way open, for instance, to the type of theory of 'communicative competence' proposed by Jürgen Habermas, a theory which Habermas carefully distinguishes from Dell Hymes's now better known notion of 'communicative competence'.[11] While Hymes's 'competence' was intended to complement Chomsky's and make up for what was seen as a deficiency in Chomsky's theory, it does not obviously yield a critical theory. The reason for this is that Hymes's theorising appears to merge Chomsky's universalistic 'competence' (a highly abstract conception of an individual's knowledge of a language reflecting the innate language capacity of *Homo sapiens*) with a relativistic conception of what it means to be able to talk (and write) appropriately in some given culture. It is certainly true that Chomsky's concept of competence does not deal with such matters; but it is arguable that it is desirable to keep the conception of universal human language ability uncoupled from culturally (and socially and politically...) determined knowledge and belief. Hymes's notion of 'appropriateness' obviously calls out for further explication. His examples are predominantly from relatively homogeneous pre-industrial cultures, but in class societies at least one cannot evade the question as to who rules (not by decree, of course, but by cultural hegemonic practices) on what is appropriate. Consider, in the light of feminist critiques of language and discourse practices,[12] one of Hymes's formulations of 'communicative competence':

> We have then to account for the fact that a normal child acquires knowledge of sentences, not only as grammatical, but also as appropriate. He or she acquires competence as to when to speak, when not, and as to what to talk about with whom, when, where, in what manner.[13]

It may not be totally fair to assert that Hymes intended the implication that a girl who interrupts a male lecturer's discourse, uses four-letter words or holds forth on motor mechanics is thereby 'incompetent'. My point is that it does not, on the other hand, entail a critique of language practices governed by specific social formations. What it does do, and for this indication we should be indebted to Hymes, is point to the existence of the *belief* amongst language users that such practices are not cultural, but natural – as natural as the ability to talk and 'grow' grammars in the first place. In other words, it points to the reification of a social practice, a social practice that in this instance happens to be carried on by means of language.

Habermas's concept is designed precisely as a yardstick for the analysis of systematic distortion in language behaviour. It is an even better complement to Chomsky's anarchist model (if that is a fair description) since it is, in Habermas's own words, 'a linguistic conceptualisation for that which we traditionally apprehend as ideas of truth, freedom and justice'.[14]

Habermas's theory, a deliberate riposte to current role-theory sociology, starts not from harmoniously integrated societies (there is something utopian about Hymes's 'normal' and 'competent' communicators), but with the existence of distortion and pathology in communication between individuals. This is not logophobia or Babelism: the focus is on what people do with language, not what language does to them – in other words, language is an instrument or tool in some underlying metaphor, not a cause. It is thus compatible with the crucial feature of Chomsky's linguistics neglected by Hymes: the creativity that enables speakers to produce a potentially infinite number of different sentences.

The difficulty in this area of linguistic speculation is to keep one's notion of creativity free of cultural determination. This was particularly the case at the time Habermas was writing in the field of semantics. It is all too easy to place the semantic structures analysed by linguists in the realm of the natural and the universal, when, as Habermas points out, they might well be products of specific cultural circumstances and world-views. Habermas thus makes an important distinction (amongst others, but we will focus on this one) between semantic universals which precede all communicative experience in individuals and those which are universal structures 'which first develop with the cultured level of linguistic communication itself'.[15] This means that theoretical semantics must reopen the question as to whether components of meaning as apparently natural as physical vs. non-physical, human vs. non-human, male vs. female, etc., would exist in the same way in the conceptual structures of animistic, religious, philosophical or scientifically oriented views of the world.

Because semantics straddles indeterminately the division between nature and culture (and that, be it noted, is itself a dichotomy not beyond question), it is not enough to explain language communication in terms of an interaction between Chomsky-type competence (an abstract system of rules) on the one hand and given situations of communication on the other – for the latter are not independently given at all, but constituted by linguistic expressions themselves. Like Hymes, therefore, Habermas insists on the necessity of positing 'communicative competence' in order to account for a speaker's ability to participate in normal discourse: 'The speaker must have – in addition to his linguistic competence – basic qualifications of speech and of symbolic interaction (role behaviour) at his disposal, which we may call communicative competence.' But where he differs from Hymes is, crucially, in concluding: 'Thus, communicative competence means the mastery of an ideal speech situation.'[16] This exactly parallels Chomsky's concept of the 'ideal speaker-hearer's' competence, and is explicitly opposed by Habermas to Hymes's use of the term 'communicative competence', which he characterises as 'sociologically limited'.

But what does Habermas mean by the 'ideal speech situation'? Is it yet another piece of linguistic utopianism, of the type we encountered in Chapter 1? According to Habermas, the ideal speech situation is an abstraction, knowledge of which must be assumed in order to explain the speakers' general ability to communicate, the potential ability to communicate in any situation 'irrespective of actual restrictions under empirical conditions'.[17] Irrespective, that is, of misfires, deceptions and specific skills of various kinds.

The 'ideal speech situation' is not presented as a utopian goal that will some day be brought to pass. Rather, Habermas is saying that communication between humans only works at all because individuals tacitly make – and expect others to make – certain assumptions of an ethical kind. These are termed 'validity claims', and Habermas gives four. First, speakers claim to be intelligible. Second, they claim to be telling the truth. Third, they claim to have some justification, right or authority to be saying what they are saying. Fourth, they claim to mean it – that is, to be sincere.

For example, if someone says 'Deterrence works', they tacitly claim that the phrase and its constituent terms are intelligible and can be explained. They claim that the assertion is factually true and can be tested in some way. They claim that they have some authority ('I am a strategic analyst', for example!) to make the assertion. They claim to be seriously intending it.

In 'undistorted communication', all four claims can be justified in discourse or demonstrated in deed. In many communicative settings, however, one cannot – or it is not done to – challenge the assumptions.

It is at this point that moral, social and political implications come to the fore, and it will be helpful to bear in mind concrete examples such as access to the media in contemporary societies and the turn-taking rights of women, children and inferiors in contemporary conversational practices.

The ideal speech situation, then, is one in which 'an unlimited inter-changeability of dialogue roles demands that no side be privileged in the performance of these roles'; here is 'complete symmetry in the distribution of assertion and disputation, revelation and hiding, prescription and following among the partners of communication'.[18] If these symmetries exist, communication will not be hindered. Habermas lists three characteristics of ideal communication. First, 'in the case of unrestricted discussion (in which no prejudiced opinion can continually avoid being made thematic and being criticised), it is possible to develop strategies for reaching unconstrained consensus'. Second, there is both freedom to express one-self and acknowledgement of others' self-expression resulting in emotional effects – the psychological integration of 'nearness' and 'inviolable distance' in acts of communication which preserve individuality. Third, 'one-sided obliging norms' will be excluded; there is 'complementation of expectations', full understanding – no participant in a dialogue imposes on any other. It is these three characteristics which, Habermas claims, give rise respectively to the linguistic conceptualisation of notions of truth, freedom and justice.

This does indeed sound like a linguistic, or communicative, utopia. But Habermas is certainly not conceiving the ideal speech situation as a utopian dream or objective. Nor does 'communicative competence' imply the capability of actually establishing the ideal speech situation. His point is that the design of an ideal speech situation is necessarily implied in the recognition of deformed or deceptive communication: all speech, even (or especially) lying, is oriented to the idea of truth.[19] It is, in Habermas's view, particular social structures at particular times which lead to specific deformations of ideal communication. The most significant contribution to a critical linguistics here is linking of political ideals (truth, freedom and justice) with communicative practices in general, and in particular with the distribution of power in dialogue between individuals, social groups, and nations. A pure communicative utopia implies a static ideal to be striven for, in which meaning is fixed and transparent. Habermas's concept of communicative competence and the ideal speech situation has two key components: it is posited as an explanation of human ability to engage in any speech encounter, and it is posited as an explanation of the ability of humans to critically recognise distortion, deception and oppression.

3

Nineteen Eighty-Four, 1984

1. Telespeak, Duckvision

There was nothing official about Newspeak in 1984; nor was there anything particularly new about it. There was nothing official, that is, in the sense of public functionaries devising new grammatical forms, coining new words and defining new meanings. It was however true that the manner of speaking and writing practised by state agencies such as the departments of 'employment', 'health', 'social security' and 'defence' – whose real business had more to do with unemployment, illness, insecurity and war – was domineering, deceptive, sometimes difficult to understand, and dependent on definitions of reality that you were expected to accept. But this stage of affairs had arisen as an automatic expression of the actual relationship between the state and the people. It was also the case that the ruling section of the population was able to hire the services of professional language manipulators to supplement its own linguistic domination, and that the newer means of electronic communication provided the means of propagating carefully packaged messages. The tacit aim of those in power was to gain popular support by circulating, through the medium of radio, television and the newspapers, a restricted set of thoughts and mental attitudes which would be consistent with their own way of seeing the world. Since speech was the key to this end, the intention was to make speech, and especially speech on any subject not ideologically neutral, as nearly as possible independent of critical consciousness. This practice ensured that the desired feelings and ideas would be received and passed around. 'You just say things frequently and people eventually understand and say it themselves' is how the marketers of Margaret Thatcher recruited from Mars (a company selling artificial food) phrased it. Duckspeak was what George Orwell had called it.

It was possible to turn off the radio set and the television screen, but it was normal for many people to keep one or the other switched on during the day and evening. In many workplaces, even in those where there was considerable noise from machinery, but especially in the quieter domestic workplace, where most women worked, the radio would throughout the day be broadcasting a continuous flow of 'news items', advertisements and other entertainments, the categories sometimes merging with one another. If you had a radio or 'telly', you were defined as a 'listener' or 'viewer', or both, and listen and view was what you felt you should do. They were, apart from the newspapers, which took up a lot of time and space, the only way of hearing about the outside world and about the decisions made by the people in remote places concerning your life and livelihood. The people who made the decisions were not 'viewed' directly, but 'inter-viewed', and even on those programmes where people 'appeared' to put questions to politicians, controls could be exercised by the 'chair person' (a popular euphemism for 'chair man'), who might wish to maintain a 'balanced view' (that is, an uncritical view), create dramatic effect, or what was professionally known as 'good television'. The television was nevertheless regarded with almost superstitious respect: to have 'seen it on the telly' was considered by many people to be a guarantee of factual truth. It is indeed possible that the term 'telly' was what linguists call a folk etymology of the incomprehensible Greek prefix *tele*: a 'telly' was a machine which told you things, like an oracle – one special service consisting of news items and other entertainments was even called by that ancient Greek name. Yet people did not ordinarily say that they had been *told* or *shown* something by the people responsible for television transmissions: they would concentrate their attention on the instrument itself, and say that they had 'watched *television*' or even 'had an evening's viewing'. And whatever other potential distractions existed, the common feeling was: you might as well watch it, you might as well get your money's worth.

It was a bright warm day in June, and the digital clock on the kitchen wall discreetly clicked 1325. Smythe jerked his way through the glass door of his living room. A face on the large television screen gazed at him with direct eyes against a background of dark blue drapes decorated with a symbolic Olympian flame supported by the corner of the Union Jack. A young woman, who was presumably his wife, was sitting with her back to him and seemed to be agreeing with everything that the face was saying. 'I think you're *so* right, I do *so* agree with you,' he heard her respond in a rather silly feminine voice. The other voice never stopped. It was rather low in pitch, reassuring, yet sporadically urgent, as if to alert anyone listening to a danger they had failed to notice. It was difficult to pick out from the stream of speech any clear proposition that might perhaps be verified by referring to observed facts, but the smooth contours of the unbroken sentences threw certain phrases into relief:

Strong in belief...resolute in our action...hold firmly together...freedom and justice...sacred flame of liberty...future belongs to free democracies...new birth of freedom...preserve our civilisation...traitors in our midst...enemy within...

What was so soothing to Smythe was the euphony of the speech, which seemed to outweigh all other considerations. The sentences were intoned without a hesitation or falter in a solid string of verbal chunks. The regularity of grammar was of no consequence: the usual means of expressing and assessing truth, likelihood, cause, the time of an event – these seemed to be unimportant and were submerged beneath the fluent rhythm. The stuff that was coming out of the mouth of the face on the television screen consisted of words, but it was not speech in the true sense: it was a noise uttered without active thought, like the quacking of a duck. It was not the brain that was speaking, it was the larynx.

And the larynx spoke to the gut, provoking the secretion of those hormones associated with courage, fear, pride and resolve. It was all done by repetition – not merely of the same words, though that was moving too, but by the repetition of bits of meaning somehow implied by words which were physically different: *strong, firm, hold.* Simultaneously, the emotions of vague collective security were stimulated: *our, together.* And in case all this evoked too static or complacent a mode, the promise of purpose and prospect was excited by bits of meaning spinning away from *action, future, new birth.* Such emotions as Smythe felt could only make sense if they were set against still stronger ones, the fear of alien forces and the will to defend one's homeland. To speak of *preserving our civilisation* made sense only if there was some threat to preserve it against, and if that threat came from some alien power, within or without, which was the very antithesis of civilisation. The threat was most effectively invoked when it was left nameless, and Smythe experienced a vague spasm of hate connected with Soviets, subversives, extremists, Marxists, militants and pacifists, none of whom could be thought of as part of the majority of decent, moderate, realistic and law-abiding people in this country. No, they *could not be thought of* in this way at all. The word *civilisation* itself was, by association rather than any grammatical link, joined to the other verbal lumps made up of nouns cemented by sound: *freedom'n'justice, freedomocracies.* They were poured forth fluently, like a line of type cast solid. There was no agreed way of defining the things these noun-lumps were presumed to be referring to, but it was widely known that they were good things, approved of by all right-thinking people, and that for the moment it was the Conservative Party that possessed them. it was also generally expected that everyone would cheer, at least inwardly, whenever they heard these words. 'Cheer' is perhaps too profane a term, because the emotion that the words were capable of arousing was almost religious. It was *belief* that was supposed to make you strong, and *a new birth* of a *sacred flame* that was meant to inspire you in a prophetic vision of the *future*.

Such curiously impressive performances, in which sight and sound could, as it were, conspire to obscure logical meaning, were not uncommon on the television screen. There were the words, combining with one another to provoke those powerful feelings. Then there was the rise and fall, the loud and soft, of that voice, pointing like a finger at important bits of speech, but also educated, confident and caring when not defiant. Then there were the gestures themselves, the stance, the distance, the dress, the angle. All carefully orchestrated in a drenching effect that could defy rational analysis.

The odd thing was, Smythe thought, the way those eyes looked constantly round the audience, while the voice never stopped to correct itself, or to allow its brain time to plan the next sentence, let alone to allow someone in the audience to interject. It could not have been reading from a script, because the eyes never looked down. For a moment Smythe wondered whether *his* brain had been mistaken, perhaps through fatigue, in not classifying this as a drama-documentary (sometimes known as 'faction') with an actor memorising a script, or perhaps as a 'commercial'. But it did not seem likely, and the only explanation was that the performer's brain was, in some sense, not at the time fully in control of what it was saying. You had the feeling, if you stopped to think about it, that this was not a real human being, but some kind of dummy. The true explanation, unknown at that time to Smythe, lay in an ingenious piece of electronic technology. It was called the 'sincerity machine', or the 'head-up device', though some technologically minded people also referred to it as the 'autocue', and it had been pioneered, as he himself would no doubt have put it, by the ageing President of Oceania, a former actor in popular films about cowboys. The thing had been admiringly adopted by the conservative Leader of Airstrip One. It consisted of a transparent plastic lectern, onto which a hidden projector cast the text of a speech. Because of the angle of the lectern the text remained invisible to everyone except the speaker and the PR ('public relations' not 'propaganda retail') experts, who controlled the device on back-stage television monitors. The speaker could read the words without looking down or hesitating – actions which were associated with weakness, uncertainty and evasiveness – while appearing to be speaking with spontaneous honesty and conviction. Even if the speaker had helped in the preparation of the content of the text, it was not necessary to think about it in the act of delivery, nor was it necessary to modify it in reaction to objections which members of the audience might have made during pauses. These seemingly minor changes in the complex of subtle signals that made up the act of communication were capable to changing the nature of political dialogue. The new smoothly produced performance conferred upon the hurly-burly of the older style of political meeting or press 'conference' a distinct dramatic quality: the speaker could now appear as a protagonist in a heroic piece of theatre on the world stage. Disbelief could be suspended. The only difference was that this was real life.

2. Unworkers, Unpersons

'This business of petty inconvenience and indignity, of being kept waiting about, of having to do everything at other people's convenience, is inherent in working-class life. A thousand influences constantly press a working man down into a *passive* role,' Orwell had written in *The Road to Wigan Pier*. Or rather an unworking man, thought Smythe, as he stood in the queue, reading Leaflet N1-12. There were a limited number of people involved-in the situation in which he found himself: 'me', 'them', 'the wife', 'the dependants', and perhaps an 'employer'; a limited number of things: 'money', 'work', 'tax'; in a limited number of places: 'the Jobcentre'; and limited (or was it to be unlimited?) periods of time: 'days', 'weeks', 'months', 'years'.

All these nouns, together with some synonyms, appeared in the leaflet, and the other words connecting them might have been expected to make quite clear the factual and logical relationships between them. But there was more than that; there was another communication, an anonymous voice addressing you, pigeon-holing you, expecting you to do things, and giving orders. That this should be so was not entirely 'their' fault, presumably. What other way was there to express these things?

It was, of course, a disembodied voice, with no visible physical source, but there was without question a process of being-spoken-to: *You Will Be Asked.* It was impossible and meaningless to ask 'by whom'? How else could it be said? It was in the nature of the relationship between the authorities and Smythe in his present position that the process should be grammatically passive. This feeling of being the powerless object of actions performed by anonymous agents grew as Smythe read. He did not act, he was acted upon. He felt himself the slave of mysterious authority; he felt that 'they' would never allow him to do this, that and the other.

> ...YOU ARE REQUIRED, YOU ARE NOT REQUIRED, YOU ARE EMPLOYED, YOU WILL BE GIVEN, YOU CAN BE SENT, YOU ARE EXPECTED...

In spite of the repeated 'you', he began to feel that he did not know who he – that is 'you' – was, any more than he knew the identity of 'them'. There was no doubt that he was the 'you' intended in the phrase 'you lose your job', but was he a 'you' who could enrol in the awesome PER? It was all very well to know what this stood for, but acronyms had a habit of taking on a life of their own. Perhaps PER was short for person, perhaps the other 'yous' were not PERsons, perhaps it stood for perhaps. Every 'you' was told that he 'should'. But was it every 'you' who was in a position to 'wish' to enrol as a PER person? It was clear that he was not the 'you under 20', the one who was given permission in the words 'you may if you wish'. The next sentence required a different kind of mental effort:

> you will not be required to register for work unless you are under 18 years old, but you can still make use of your local Jobcentre.

This was not perhaps as difficult to decipher as the sentence 'it is not the case that negative sentences are not harder to understand than affirmatives', but it did take more time to make sense of than saying 'if you are over 18 you will not be required, etc... if you are under 18, you will be required, etc.'. The latter translation would at least have made it plain what they were demanding.

The well-dressed woman in front of Smythe was sweating slightly. Was she a 'you', he asked himself. It occurred to him that 'you' was in itself normally genderless, but could turn masculine or feminine depending on surrounding words, a bit like some nouns. 'Neighbour', for example became feminine when you said 'My neighbour is pregnant', and so it did, for slightly different reasons, if you said 'My neighbour is doing the washing'. He had a feeling that you in the Ubo was always assumed to be masculine. 'If your wife stops working,' spoke the voice in the leaflet, although there was no knowing that this *you* could be any different from the *you* in the other sentences. If she stops working, what then? 'You...claim extra benefit *for her*,' replied the voice. If both husband and wife were out of work, then the man claimed. But what if a woman was unemployed and unmarried? What, for the matter of that, if she was married? The voice did not, apparently, speak to such persons.

The queue was moving slowly, and Smythe preferred this game to chess problems. The first sentence now said, 'you [man] *lose your job*', the later one 'your wife *stops working*'. Wives who stopped working were, it now seemed, part of some uncontrollable thing happening, which was referred to as 'your [men's] circumstances chang[ing]'. Smythe's pulse quickened as he glimpsed still more possible messages; the train of his thoughts was, he knew, unacceptable, unreasonable, but he did not stop short. 'You lose your job...your wife stops working'. Lose: did that mean lose like losing an arm, or lose like losing your hat, by being damn careless? At any rate, it implied you didn't intend to do it, because English didn't normally let you say 'He lost his hat, as he intended'. So 'intend' wasn't normally part of 'lose'. Nor did it normally let you say 'She stopped walking, but did not intend to'. So 'intend' *was* part of 'stop'. It seemed that they expected 'you' [man] would become unemployed because something happened (even though you might be blamed for being lazy, stupid or imprudent), while wives 'stopped working', because ... well, because they intended to, wanted to. You men were expected to have a job; your wives could, it was implied, choose whether they had one or not. It also occurred to him, as he allowed his thoughts to drift, that if you did think of 'stop working' as something just happening, then you had to think of the wife as a kind of mechanical gadget that had ceased to function.

A shuffling in the queue brought him back to the question of his relationship to 'them'. The leaflet's big-brotherly voice said, although somehow without saying it, that Smythe, the woman in front and every you in the Ubo was to take the role of receiving orders (as well as 'benefits'): *Go...give...do not delay* (there was a recurrent emphasis on punctuality and timekeeping that seemed to reflect some conception of a worker's or unworker's duties): *fill it in...return it quickly...ask...read it...make sure...follow...tell the benefit office everything you are required to*, commanded the voice.

There was also a prediction of Smythe's future actions in the office, a prediction which he knew he must fulfil: 'Each time you claim benefit, you will sign that you have read and understood UBL 18. So read it...' Not only would he sign, he *would* read, and he *would* understand, if he was going to sign, he *must* be going to read, he *must* be going to understand. He longed for this understanding. The woman was already reading the inside of UBL 18, and on its front page Smythe saw: *So you must tell us at once. You must tell us immediately.* Imperatives, which after all are just verbs with ɔu suppressed, are full of power, mused Smythe, beginning to penetrate the labyrinthine language game; just like questions, which most people feel obliged to answer, though statements of your future actions are even more compelling.

What else could you, and they, do with verbs? Evidently it was possible to do more than merely refer to actions and the like. If imperatives were anything to go by, you ought to be able to indicate whether an action was enforced or permitted, by someone assuming the power to enforce or permit, whether it was possible or impossible, real or unreal, likely or unlikely. Smythe had not thought of cans, mights, mays, woulds and shoulds in quite this light before, but those were clearly the words involved. Sometimes the distinction between having the ability to do something and being allowed to do it was not very clear in this system: sometimes it depended on the sentence. The effect of *can* and *cannot* when the subject was a thing was to ascribe an inherent potential to that thing, rather than to ascribe it to the person acting on that thing. *Payment* cannot *be backdated*: it was just one of those petty inconveniences about payments. *You* can *be sent to prison* meant, of course that, *we (or they) can send you*, but they wrote it so that it seemed to be just one of those inherent inconveniences about *you*. They had another way of implying what they thought about you, which made use of bits of sentence beginning with *if*: *if you tell a lie*, for instance, seemed to suppose that you were likely to.

Almost all of the verbs, Smythe noticed, had a can, may or might carefully connected to them, presumably to avoid definite commitment on the part of the authorities. This was scarcely reassuring, since any apparent offer of rights was instantly hedged. Even if it was 'very difficult' for you to 'attend' the Ubo ('attendance' was a duty normally expected of church-goers and schoolchildren), the most they offered was that *you* may *be able to claim by post*. Could Smythe, who had cycled ten miles and left his small son with a neighbour, have stayed at home or not? 'If you don't claim' (another supposition that you might forget or be too feckless to fill in the form), it was not clear what might happen: *you* may *lose your money*. Only they could decide.

The obligations of the Ubo certainly weren't clear, but what, he wondered, were *his* obligations? Smythe read the front page of UBL 18 with difficulty, as he and the woman moved toward the counter: *Responsibilities of Claimants*.

This leaflet tells you, said the institutional voice.

Read it...if you break the rules [as you are likely to], you *may* be breaking the law... These are the rules, but if you are not sure whether you should *tell* us about something, *tell* us anyway, just in case. You should read it and remember...

He should have known, of course, that the general rules would be indicated, but not the law, for what counted was right thinking. One should have not only the right opinions, but the right instincts. Yes, he would tell big brother all, he would tell him that he had read and understood, and that he had also not understood; he would tell him that he filled his memory with with do's, don'ts, coulds and shoulds, but that at the end of it all he knew only that he must *tell*. But he had already gone too far. He was losing the faculty of stopping short at the threshold of dangerous thoughts, the power of *not* grasping analogies; he was forgetting how to *fail* to perceive logical errors, how to *mis*understand the simplest arguments that were not 'moderate', he was forgetting how to be bored or repelled by trains of thought which were not sensible, reasonable and orthodox.

4

What is Newspeak?

The rhetorical techniques for influencing and controlling others were probably first widely developed in Europe in the Greek democracies. In the 1980s they are no longer studied and mostly go unnoticed, and any attempts to raise them to consciousness risk being laughed off stage by those who stand most to gain by them ('mere semantics', 'academic', 'splitting hairs', 'just rhetoric'...). The invention of print made it easier to manipulate public opinion. Film and the radio have carried the process further. And the development of television and other forms of electronic communication meant that the process could be carried further still. Verbal communication, together with various forms of visual communication, is probably more pervasive and persuasive than ever before.

In some respects, Newspeak – in the sense of a new politically planned form of the existing language – was unnecessary in 1984. Accents, grammar and the daily uses to which language was put already expressed, defined and reinforced the social hierarchy in the British Isles. The sociologist Basil Bernstein (not to be confused with the fictional Emmanuel Goldstein of *Nineteen Eighty-Four*) is well known for his attempts to theorise the differences in linguistic practice between working-class and middle-class speakers of English, and his work, especially as interpreted by teachers and educational theorists, has caused much confusion of the question.[1] It is not primarily a matter of accent (that is, of pronunciation), although the matter of accent deserves comment, because of its role in broadcasting, and because to many people it is the most obvious aspect of linguistic conflict. Subtle variations in accent correspond to subtle regional and class distinctions. One accent, which itself possessed its own variations (reflecting, among other things, one's age and the school one attended), has become socially dominant. Historically linked with the accent of the economically dominant South-East, it is the accent of power, prestige and authority in all regions of England and Wales. From early on it was the accent of broadcasting: anyone who speaks it tends to be regarded as more reliable and intelligent than someone who does not, even if they are speaking the same words and sentences. Its superiority is rationalised in various ways, by being called 'purer' or 'less slovenly'. It can affect your prospects of employment if, for example, in saying the word *class* you hold your tongue further forward for the vowel than someone who speaks the approved accent, or if you neglect to cause friction in your throat in saying the first part of *'orrible*, although the likelihood of being misunderstood is not great. One's particular accent does not necessarily entail a vocabulary and grammar different from what is called 'standard' English. If it does, however, you are generally said to be speaking 'in a dialect', not just 'with an accent', and your social status is usually deemed as being correspondingly lower. Many people can, of course, vary their accent, and their dialect as well, if they have one, to suit the occasion, but this does not necessarily mean that conflict is not present either within or between individuals.

These curious but revealing tongue habits were not, however, the main concern of Bernstein's theories. What was at issue was not so much the sounds, words and grammar of the proles as opposed to the rest, but the different ways in which the proles *used* their language. Proles have been believed by many who have read Bernstein to speak a 'restricted code', and some people have believed that in consequence they must have restricted minds. The educated, it was claimed, tended to speak an 'elaborated code'. In fact, these beliefs are probably misinterpretations of Bernstein, who has not always been sufficiently explicit in his writings. There are indeed differences in language use between the classes – differences between what you are *in a position* to say if you are well-housed, well-fed, well-travelled, employed and powerful, and what you are in a position to say if you are not some or all of these things. But the distinction between 'restricted' and 'elaborated' code *could* apply to both low and high social strata: both working class and middle classes use both codes *sometimes*, but on different occasions and for different purposes. 'Restricted code' is supposed to be the use of simple sentences, limited and inexplicit means of referring to things, lack of abstractions and lack of self-reference. Bernstein thought that working-class children used it in schools, where 'elaborated code' was expected, and thus did poorly; he also seemed to think that 'restricted code' led to restricted ability to form concepts. Others have sometimes deduced from this that working-class children suffer from something termed 'cognitive deficiency'. This label has been popular with American educational experts, who gain by the technical and medical ring of the phrase, and by the fact that if someone is deficient in something, a 'remedy' seems to be required: and if a 'remedy' is required, then so is a specialist professional. Such notions have perhaps been merely a way of asserting control over the working class, by increasing the control of the educational system over them through 'remedial' action. 'Elaborated code', which middle-class people were thought to speak *in addition* to 'restricted code', was supposed to possess all the qualities lacking in 'restricted code'; they were therefore not, it was assumed, likely to be cognitively lacking.

Orwell's *Nineteen Eighty-Four* has, as Fowler and Hodge[2] point out, a somewhat similar, yet crucially distinct, schema to the one embodied in Bernstein's work. Orwell's Newspeak looks very like Bernstein's 're-stricted code' in certain respects: reduced complexity, few abstractions, no self-reference which could create the conditions for self-criticism. But Newspeak in the novel is a restricted code that is peculiar to the ruling class; the proles do not speak it. Its purpose was to provide a medium of expression for the world-view and mental habits of the ruling elite, and also to make all other modes of thought impossible. If it had an equivalent in real-time 1984, it was to be found in the rhetoric of party politics, the bureaucratic prose of the agents of the state, and the arcane incantations of those who are cast in the role of 'experts'. No one can force you to speak or write it, but the printing and broadcasting of it can leave you with no choice (other than not reading or listening at all) but to read it or listen to it for certain purposes; in addition, there is a degree of pressure to use it yourself, in order to communicate economically in the idiom of the day with others who have been exposed to it.

The political scientist Murray Edelman has elucidated the political role of the Bernstein dichotomy.[3] Bernstein is wrong, he argues, to correlate an 'elaborated' (or 'formal') language with class level,[4] and sees the cruder formulations of this view as a classification scheme with two political functions: to reinforce the consignment of people to different levels of merit; and to justify controls over them. He does not, however, jettison the distinction between 'elaborated' (or 'formal') language and 'restricted' (or 'public') language, which he believes to be useful in comprehending the strategic use of language in political life, where both codes are blended by the state and its agencies. Formal, elaborated language, in Edelman's view, is capable of calling attention to factual allegations and logical relationships, and of expressing alternative views of reality. Public language, on the other hand, 'rather than abstracting formal elements that can be reordered to yield new possibilities...validates established beliefs and strengthens the authority structure of the polity or the organisation in which it is used'.[5] It tends to be a 'tough' language, discouraging the verbalisation of tender (or 'wet') feelings. It takes many forms, of which the appeal to patriotism and support for the leader and her or his regime are but the most obvious.

The basic tendency of restricted public language in Edelman's sense is the closing off of discourse, by allowing only certain topics to be discussed (often these topics have the character of myth), by obscuring reference to process, causation and responsibility, and by disallowing criticism. These ends are achieved by linguistic means: the choice and creation of a certain type of vocabulary, the choice of inexplicit grammatical constructions, and the use of certain tactics when communicating with others. It may seem strange that anyone should get away with such things; and so it is. The fact is, however, that the political culture of 1984, underpinned by the press and the electronic media, privileges a certain *voice*. It does not liquidate or lock up dissenting voices, and for that one is thankful, but it is none the less effective in legitimating the structures of power.

The nature of this *Institutional Voice* (IV) has been analysed by Claire Lindegren Lermen, who has given the term *Topic Transformation* to its techniques of reality control.[6] The IV does not speak in its own personal capacity, but distances itself from the person 'I', and equates itself with its office or role, rather like the royal 'we'. It identifies its policies with 'the good of all', 'national security', 'public interest', 'our way of life', and so forth, and thereby tends to squeeze out factual examination of premises. The IV depends on unspoken and almost magical conventions which it is taboo to challenge publicly: it alone has the right to speak for the nation or institution; it is the repository of power and tradition; and it makes a unique claim to virtue, a claim which it recurrently insists upon. It has thus the ability to define events and people, and to assign a moral value to them. There are two key domains in this defining process: what and who poses a threat (that is, what and who we should fear) and what constitutes safety (that is, who and what belongs and is patriotic). The IV accomplishes this by transforming the topics of discourse: modifying or suppressing irksome political topics, like unemployment, the nuclear arms race, the objectives behind the Falklands war. Its most powerful linguistic tools are much like those of Edelman's public language, but can now be spelled out in more detail: (i) the choice of grammatical constructions that avoid explicit reference to causes, agents, time and place; (ii) the preference for and production of particular words and metaphors, which hide some aspects of reality and heighten others; (iii) the invitation to draw inferences as a consequence of (i) and (ii), evoking wider patterns of unspoken belief. All three of these linguistic practices are exemplified in what follows.

'It's a beautiful thing, the destruction of words.' So said Syme, who was working on the crude dictionary of Newseak. In 1984 topic control is subtler, but the aim is the same. 'Don't you see that the whole aim of Newspeak is to narrow the range of thought?'.[7] The campaign against CND in 1983 involved the systematic attempt to replace the term 'unilateral' in public debate with the term 'one-sided', with its implication of intellectual and moral limitations.

The ultimate achievement for the IV would be to get its vocabulary imperceptibly incorporated into popular usage. The word *deterrent* is almost such a case. It has long been assimilated into public usage, and encapsulates a whole ideology based on the simultaneous evocation of threat and reassurance. The form of the word gives it a technical connotation and therefore a kind of authority (cf. ag*ent*, reag*ent*, dispers*ant*...). It is also relevant that words with this form can be euphemisms (like defoli*ant* in the Vietnam war) or serve commercial ends (like deterg*ent* and deodor*ant*). But what is most important is that the term *deterrent* carries unspoken implications: (i) it says, in ʿnilitary contexts, 'nuclear', without saying it aloud; (ii) it asserts, as if it were a fact, that A deters B, without giving the listener a chance to question the truth of the assertion in relation to the past, present or future; (iii) it says that B is aggressive; and (iv) that A is non-aggressive and even benevolent, because opposed to an aggressor. So the word *deterrent* asserts the presence of an alien threat while at the same moment asserting the ability to ward it off. It is thus a potent symbol for attracting political allegiance, whose usefulness becomes clear in the course of public debate. For to say 'It is wrong to want to get rid of the deterrent' is almost self-evidently true, if you take for granted, as the word encourages you to, that there does indeed exist some thing x such that x prevents y from attacking z.

Why should we consider it a coincidence that the other domains in which the word *deterrent* is used are those of public order (the 'rope') and school discipline (the 'cane')? Nonetheless, it is not possible to use the phrase 'the deterrent' and mean 'hanging'; one still has to say 'I believe hanging to be *a* deterrent'. And belief, *a priori* and irrational, is what motivates the proponents of such a view, since the penal evidence for the effectiveness of this 'deterrent' is fairly clearly negative. Belief in the two deterrents, the rope and the bomb, is symmetrical and intimately related. The one wards off internal fear and the fear of disorder, the other external evil and the fear of invasion.

The link between the two can sometimes surface in curious ways in the media – ways which suggest how strongly defence and domestic policy are intertwined at the back of some minds. An article with the telling title 'The Front Line against Youth Unemployment' (*Daily Telegraph*, 19 July 1982) treats the problem of unemployment as an internal evil to be 'combatted'. (Another common metaphor for unemployment is that of *disease*: 'the cancer of unemployment'). The noun 'unemployment,' now well entrenched in our usage, is itself highly revealing. Both 'employment' and 'unemployment' act as abstract nouns, and obscure the fact that what is denoted is not a thing, but a process and an economic relationship between people. Also, while 'employment' can refer to a process (A employs B), *unemployment* (A unemploys B?) does not. There is no simple single-word way of distinguishing between voluntary unemployment and unemployment *tout court*, and this fact is often exploited. There is no way of distinguishing between A who un-employed him – or her self, as it were, and A who was un-employed by B. If the un-employed are responsible for their own un-employment, then the simple logic of the prefix implies that they must be disciplined, even punished, back into employment.

The 'front line' in question turns out to be a secondary modern school for girls in Chatham, and the ensuing discourse shows how subtle (and not so subtle) linguistic cues can trigger off interconnected beliefs concerning the economy, defence and public order. 'We are trying', declared the headmistress, a Mrs Dagger, 'to turn out [the pupils are products of an assembly line, you see] the sort of people who will exhibit [not really *have*, of course] middle-class notions of what is acceptable [to whom?] and marketable.' The author of the article also comments: 'It's the schools who are marketing a product.' Now the metaphor 'headmistress' was not applied to the Prime Minister in 1984 for nothing; nor are war, work and school, captains of companies, captains of industry and captains of schools, verbally connected for nothing. For in the Chatham girls' school marketing is a military operation, and teaching is indoctrination. 'Economic war' justifies the draconian measures. 'Part of the process [the education of children is the "processing of products"] is simple, unrelenting [this word is second-cousin to "resolute"] *brainwashing* ...' The senior master, described by the article's author as 'the market economy made flesh', has more powerful 'weapons' at his disposal, however. There is an interesting progression from seeing education as an industrial process to seeing it as psychological warfare and then as physical warfare. The military-industrial-educational complex, in fact. The 'brainwashing', we are told, is backed up by a considerable range of minor punishments up to '*nuclear weapons*'. The function of the senior master's deterrent seems to be to brainwash children into accepting the market economy. We may have here the key to a whole pattern of thought.

Such things can be laughed off (like the 'comedian' at the Conservative rally of 1983 shouting 'Let's bomb the Russians' and 'Let's kick Michael Foot's stick away'). And the article *could* be taken as satire.

But suppose it is not: vocabulary, metaphor and implications all work to organise a highly partial view of reality. The discourse is built round the threat or fear of unemployment; that is linked with the fear of youth and domestic disorder; and this in turn with the fear of an alien threat. The unifying and wholly irrational resolution to this cluster of phobias is the symbol of the 'deterrent' as safeguard and discipline.

The cuing of such patterns of belief is dispersed through media messages, but the speaker is none the less the Institutional Voice. Its operations are more obvious in the face-to-face utterances studied by Lerman. In a radio interview (BBC Radio 4, 17 April 1980), the Prime Minister demonstrated the control and definition of the topic of trade unions, closing the discourse off from interactive discussion and challange.

> I'm not afraid of the trade unions [breath] which carry out the true idea of trade unions, which is to get a fair return for the members ...and to help to raise the prosperity of the country...
> Because the *fact is* that the only group of people in this country who are above the law in some respect is the trade unions...
> Indeed the majority of them [trade union members] don't like it. We want to reduce the power of *the militants* in the trade unions to use the union to *their* advantage, and not to the advantage of the country.[8]

The IV conventionally has the right to make truth claims. Hence 'the true ideal ... *is*', 'the only group ... *is*, 'indeed', and, above all, 'the fact *is*.' In fact a frequent feature of this speaker's discourse is the expression 'you know', implying superior knowledge on her part. The IV defines threats to the national security. Hence the unions are represented as something of which one might be afraid, though simultaneously the IV reassuringly asserts its own fearlessness. It is implied that there exist false unions, distinct from the 'true' ones (in 1983, ministers also made claims about the '*true* peace movement'); they are 'the militants', they have 'power' that they use 'not to the advantage of the country'. The IV claims virtue as well as the truth: it knows what is 'fair'. Typically it claims to know 'public opinion' and to be aligned with it: 'the majority of them'.

The IV's control of difficult topics by appeals to national security and patriotism was clearly seen when it was questioned on an untypical television programme during the election 'campaign' (elections are always treated as if they were military campaigns) of 1983. The difficult topic was whether it had been necessary during the Falklands war of 1982 to torpedo an Argentinian cruiser called the *General Belgrano*. Being dissatisfied with the Prime Minister's evasive answer, a questioning member of the electorate committed the unpardonable fault of challenging the IV's virtue and veracity by saying, 'That's not good enough, Mrs Thatcher.'ᐧ To this the IV replied by side-stepping the difficult topic and transforming it into an indirect assertion of the identity between the IV's actions and the national interest: '... only in England could anybody question the sinking of an enemy ship', which suppressed reference to time, place and cause, while presenting the event as a timeless phenomenon beyond moral questioning.

The Falklands war of 1982 was indeed a case where the IV, with the support of the media, effectively ruled criticism of that war off-side, together with any perception of the links between that war and the economic and political situation at home. This is not to say that 'free speech' itself was suppressed, merely that dissent was drowned by the Institutional Voice. The war itself was not necessary; it was a symbol in political discourse. 'The war', wrote Orwell's Goldstein, 'though it is unreal is not meaningless. It eats up the surplus of consumable goods, and it helps to preserve the typical mental atmosphere that a hierarchical society needs ... the object of war is not to make or prevent conquests of territory, but to keep the structure of society intact.'[9] Preventing conquest of territory was precisely the ostensible aim for the Falklands war. Yet the real function of this claim was to enable the IV to assert its own rightness by invoking an alien threat, and by branding as 'traitors' people who voiced objections. Beyond this, it had the function of defining traditional roles and hierarchies. This was done largely through metaphors. War could be seen as *work* ('just doing one's job'); reciprocally, the world of work could be seen as entailing a kind of warfare (against 'union militants' and the unemployment and inflation for which they were represented as being responsible). Government and media rhetoric at the time of the railwaymen's strike, which occurred shortly after the war, was a mirror image of Falklands rhetoric.[10]

We opened this chapter by referring to verbal techniques for influencing or controlling thought. There are, of course, outside linguistic science fiction, no such sure-fire weapons. What the above examples show is not the power of a neo-Newspeak absolutely and inevitably to control thought. They show, rather, that in political discourse language is used to define and redefine reality to the advantage of a dominant ideology. It may be that many people are induced to accept some or all of the messages conveyed, but that is not a necessary consequence. Thought and language are not necessarily identical. What is more, language has the peculiar property of being able to refer to itself, potentially to the nth degree, so that any linguistically realised version of reality is capable of turning on itself.

5

What is Nukespeak?

Since the first atomic bomb destroyed Hiroshima, each new twist of the arms race has been accompanied by a new twist in official propaganda and disinformation. Post-Hiroshima culture has, moreover, had to create for itself new images and vocabulary to encapsulate the inconceivable, to neutralise and naturalise a potential for destruction of an order beyond previous human experience, and possibly beyond ordinary human conception. The development of atomic fission weapons was not a smooth progression from existing weaponry, but a catastrophic jump to a new order of experience in science, politics and everyday life. (In 1945 it was popular to refer to it as a 'revolution' that would itself 'revolutionise' human action.) The nuclear fusion weapons were yet another jump. To communicate about matters on the fringe of experience and imagination places strain on our symbolic systems. The language used to talk about the new weapons of mass extermination was, in part, a reflection of an attempt to slot the new reality into the old paradigms of our culture. It was also a language that served the purposes of those who had an interest in maintaining nuclear weapons developments, in getting populations to accept their existence, and even to accept their possible use. Anyone born since 1940 will have grown up exposed to this language; many will have learnt to speak it; and most will regard it as being as natural as English itself.

The current propaganda battle has generated many speeches, pamphlets and books on all sides. There have been various techniques of persuasion, appeals to emotion, morality and reason, but crucial to any rational debate is the provision of accurate information about the material base of the superpower conflict. While some people have attempted to illuminate the facts about military-industrial substructures, to unveil the effects of nuclear explosions, to expose civil 'defence' planning, the main polemic thrust has been the Numbers Game, that is, the (usually tendentious) comparison of the superpowers' nuclear arsenals. The present essay does not seek to contribute to any of these areas, but rather to look more closely at the Word Game, the game played by the nuclear nations in order to manipulate and mystify the material facts. This word game as played in English I have called *nukespeak*.

To coin the term *nukespeak* is to make the claim that talk about nuclear weapons, nuclear war and nuclear politics is carried on by means of distinctive words and phrases, and that this *in itself* has important consequences for thought and action concerning those matters. (Of course, there are visual means at work too.) There seem to be two main ways of considering such consequences. One is to treat *nukespeak* as the symptom of nuclear culture, as an indication of the depth of its penetration into our mentality: 'The deformation of culture commences within language itself. It makes possible a disjunction between the rationality and moral sensibility of individual men and women and the effective political and military process. A certain kind of "realist" and "technical" vocabulary effects a closure which seals out the imagination, and prevents the reason from following the most manifest sequence of cause and consequence. It habituates the mind to nuclear holocaust by reducing everything to a flat level of normality. By habituating us to certain expectations, it not only encourages resignation – it also beckons on the event'.[1] To approach nukespeak in this light may be to increase our awareness of 'the hideous cultural abnormalities'[2] to which we have become accustomed, and to free ourselves from their constraining assumptions.

The second way of considering the consequences of nukespeak is to consider it primarily as a form of social control, as means of setting limits on possible thought and action. One important way in which such limits are set is the suppression of information by and through the media, but it is not my aim to follow this up here. Rather I am concerned with the manner of what *is* told, with the way language is exploited to influence the way people think and feel about nuclear matters.

An important reservation needs to be made. Nukespeak exists because of prevailing socio-economic relations, because of a particular distribution of power in the communicating institutions, and because of the nature of superpower politics. In understanding nukespeak we change nothing. But by becoming conscious of it we may be able to demystify it, cease to regard it as natural and normal, and challenge the forces that produce it. We may be able to recognise the capacity of nukespeak for limiting the range of conceivable ideas and for subtly influencing people to think favourably of nuclear weapons and nuclear strategy. Though no substitute for political action as such, to challenge the ideological assumptions inherent in a language or some variety of language is probably more of a political act than some might suppose.

Human languages are complex systems for the communicating of immensely subtle effects of meaning. Any speaker wishing to influence or coerce another person can exploit their language in various ways in order to do so. It would be possible to classify the exploitative techniques. Rather than do that, however, it seems more relevant to approach three major questions. Who makes nukespeak, and why? In what ways does nukespeak come to terms with and create a post-Hiroshima nuclear mythology? And in what ways is language manipulated when the nuclear establishment seeks to persuade the public?

To be sure that it makes sense to postulate a variety of English that we can call nukespeak, we need to ask whether it *matters* what variety of language one speaks. There are numerous obvious ways in which it *can* be said to matter both socially and politically. Accent and dialect can be used to exercise power, for example. But can we claim anything stronger? Can we claim that even wording and phrasing determine to any extent the way people think, feel and even act?

In *Nineteen Eighty-Four*, George Orwell creates the idea of *Newspeak*, the official language of Big Brother's totalitarian state: 'The purpose of Newspeak was not only to provide a medium of expression for the world-view and mental habits proper to the devotees of Ingsoc [the dominant ideology], but to make all other modes of thought impossible. It was intended that when Newspeak had been adopted ... a thought diverging from the principles of Ingsoc should be literally unthinkable, at least as far as thought is dependent on words.'

The assumptions behind all this seem to be that it is not only possible to coerce people into using a prescribed set of linguistic forms, but also that such forms will determine the thoughts they can think. These are dubious assumptions, as is the assumption that all thought is dependent on language in the first place. The view that the language you speak necessarily determines the way you think is known as the 'Whorfian hypothesis' (after the American linguist B.L. Whorf). It represents a notoriously difficult claim, and is worth looking at more closely, not least because the claim itself has serious political implications. If your language did totally determine and delimit the thoughts you could think, it ought in theory to be impossible for you to understand the thought of someone who speaks an entirely different language. This is evidently not the case, since it is possible to translate meanings from one language to another, even if paraphrase is needed. To take a pertinent example, it is often said that the Russians don't have a word for *deterrent*. That is, they do not have a single word simultaneously expressing meanings like 'inspiring fear' and 'holding back an aggressor'. This does not mean they cannot paraphrase the notion quite adequately. It may merely mean that they have less need or less desire to combine those particular meanings with each other. But the Whorfian assumption can lead to some extremely unhelpful conclusions. In an illuminating article P. Vigor concludes: 'This failure to be able to express in Russian the essential notion [why 'essential', incidentally?] of the concept "to deter" has naturally been reflected in a similar failure to express correctly in Russian either "deterrent" or "deterrence".' In other words, *'The Russian mind is particularly ill-equipped to apprehend the notion of the "act of deterring" and not much better to apprehend that of "the thing that deters"* ... And from this it has followed, until very recently, that, by the sheer clumsy mechanics of the phrases they have been forced to use, real debate on "deterrence" between Russians was bound to be a remarkably clumsy business. *One cannot think clearly with tangled knots of verbiage* ... This must inevitably have hindered the evolution in the Soviet Union of a proper discussion, *and hence of a proper understanding, of the concept of deterrence'*(Emphasis added).[3]

There may be some grains of truth here concerning ease and economy of discussion. But you need to believe in the first place that the concept of 'deterrence' is absolutely valid, or that it is relevant and important for the population of speakers in question; as a matter of fact, Vigor also states that 'the Russians *need* [his emphasis] to have a meaningful debate about deterrence'. But it is also Vigor's conclusion that the Russian mind cannot think 'deterrence' because it can't say 'deterrence'. Vigor's conclusions, however, are not really logical inferences at all but assumptions or prejudices that can only be described as ideological in origin. First, it is assumed that 'deterrence' is a useful and valid, indeed an 'essential', concept. Perhaps Vigor believes this merely because the word *deterrence* exists – the Whorfian approach rebounds at that point, and we shall return to the matter in a later section. Secondly, there is a failure to see, or to admit, that Russian linguistic habits are interesting for a different reason: the fact that Russians don't talk to one another about their 'nuclear deterrent' but often designate their nuclear rockets as 'the primary defence force' should say something about their concern with, or concern to express, fear of aggression. (This does not justify or excuse *actual* aggressive or menacing acts; it merely helps to comprehend Russian attitudes or poses.) Thirdly, the linguistic evidence (such as it is) is being used to bolster some crude stereotypes of 'the enemy': among other things it is implied that they are 'clumsy', cannot 'think clearly' and are even slightly stupid. (We shall return to other myths about the Russian 'mind' and the supposed attempts of 'the West' to get inside it in later sections.) Fourthly, Vigor assumes not only that they are unable to communicate with Western negotiators, but that they make no attempt to do so. In fact, the 'clumsy paraphrases' cited by Vigor are used by Soviet experts when trying to find a common language with Western writers. That they lack the status of technical terms in Soviet military science could and should be taken as a useful clue to the way Russians do talk, and possibly think, about nuclear matters.[4] In short, Vigor's article, which parades as academic linguistics, far from furthering understanding of the Soviet outlook through an analysis of their language, merely records a rigid refusal to entertain any system of values other than those embodied in English, or, more specifically, in that variety of English we are calling nukespeak.

The point I wish to make is that the extreme Whorfian claim (that the language you speak determines the limits of your possible thoughts) is not tenable, even if it is convenient for some types of argument (such as the one we've just been considering) to believe that it is. Vigor's claims are an example of how not to use the Whorfian hypothesis – against others, but ignoring the corollary that if it applies to others it must apply to you too. In a later section we shall look more closely at what effect the word and concept 'deterrence' may have on its users.

There are other lines of argument that tend to undermine the view that language determines thought, and I shall mention two briefly. One is that if a language or some sub-variety (like nukespeak) did determine what thoughts, including values, you could hold, then it would be impossible to get outside the system and criticise it. Another is that psychological research strongly suggests that many basic concepts (colour, for instance, despite the fact that, superficially, colour vocabularies vary) are determined biologically and not by the particular language of speakers.[5] In spite of all this, it would be rash to jettison Orwell's original insight – that language can be used in some way to control thought (particularly where ideology is concerned). To quote an eminent researcher in the psychology of language: 'Speech is the most subtle and powerful instrument we have for controlling other people. Nothing that psychologists can invent in their laboratories is likely to be nearly as influential in controlling people.'[6] Such control may have to do with the authority of the person speaking, and other non-linguistic factors, but speech seems intuitively to have a strangely compulsive power. People respond when called, answer questions thrown at them, listen to statements when made, even if they do not want to.[7] Now clearly it is not *impossible* for people to think through or round the pre-coded concepts of their language; nor is it *impossible* for them to resist the compulsiveness of individual speech acts; nor is it the case that *all* aspects of language structure are relevant to the determination, influence or control of thought. However, it *is* possible that some speakers, probably many speakers, will *not* think round the language they use in some contexts, and that they will *not* resist the demands of specific speech acts. Similarly it *is* probably the case that certain elements of vocabulary and grammar are implicated directly in affecting attitudes and concepts. Instead of making absolute claims about the *necessary* determination of *all* thought by *all* aspects of language, it is more useful to ask which parts of language influence which speakers, in which contexts and to what degree. The fact is that speakers and hearers of language vary considerably in their performance. Diverse factors like attention, verbal skill and ideological background will affect the extent to which they are able or willing to question assumptions coded in language; some may do so to a considerable degree, but since you cannot be on top of language all the time, many people will be unquestioning in many contexts. This is something one can begin to change by looking at a sub-variety like nukespeak.

Much of the difficulty raised by the Whorfian hypothesis can be cut through if, instead of focussing on the relation between language and thought, we focus on the relation between individuals and groups in communicative exchange. People communicate with one another by means of whatever verbal tokens are to hand. When they talk on a particular topic, be it nuclear weapons or the weather, they draw on a pre-existing fund of words in order to refer to the objects, processes, etc., that interest them. They are not totally bound in the ideas they can swap (since there is great freedom in the way words can be combined), but to some extent they are. The American linguist, Dwight Bollinger, puts it as follows: 'The words we use are the words that are *there*; we can only choose from them, rarely invent them, and if they are not clean to begin with, the precision – not to mention the honesty – of our message will suffer.'[8] But this is not the whole story. There are two sets of additional questions that might be posed. First, what does it mean to say that the words are 'there'? They surely cannot be natural objects of spontaneous growth. And who are 'we' that have not 'invented' them? If 'we' have not invented them, who has? For a language as a whole these may be difficult if not impossible questions. But they acquire a great deal of sense if asked of subvarieties of a language handling specific domains of experience, like nukespeak. Second, there is the related question of the way verbal tokens relate to, correspond to, match the world they are supposed to describe. (Words do other things as well, of course, like relating things logically, spatially, temporally, and expressing emotion, etc., but that is not the main issue for the moment.) Is there any reason why a particular combination of sounds or letters should stand for a particular object? Is there, looking at it the other way round, any particular reason why objects, etc., should be isolated by attaching verbal tags to them?

To take the last set of questions first, language is clearly not just a copy of reality, a list of names each of which corresponds to a thing. The world is not just a collection of neatly ordered separate objects waiting to have their labels attached. Anyone who has learnt a foreign language knows that different languages carve up the world in different ways. English, for example, carves out the set of things called *rivers*, while French obliges you to subdivide the set into *fleuves* (flowing into the sea) and *rivieres* (flowing into other rivers). English can conveniently let you classify things as either *blue* or *green*, while Welsh conflates the two as *glas*. These are relatively inconsequential examples: the words don't prevent people from perceiving the distinctions involved or from expressing them by means of paraphrase. They may, however, since it is more convenient to use available single words than to invent paraphrases, affect which ideas are actually talked about and exchanged. This may not have much significance as far as colours and rivers are concerned, but if the same kind of situation holds for economic, social and political life, it is not difficult to see that the consequences could be very interesting. If, for example, nuclear research and development, nuclear strategy, nuclear diplomacy, constitute an erea of reality 'carved up' in a particular fashion by a certain static nexus of words and phrases, and if there is pressure to use that vocabulary exclusively, then there may well be certain limits on what people can *talk* about, even if there are not limits on what they can (given the time and inclination) *think* about.

To see how this could be the case, we can return to the question of the relationship between letters/sounds and their combinations. Except for onomatopoeic effects, the connection between the sounds/letters of words and their meanings is *arbitrary*: i.e. while words like *woofer* and *tweeter* are perhaps linked to the things they denote by their very sound, words like *table*, *chair*, *weapon*, *war*, are not. The things they refer to *could* be denoted by different words of different sound and appearance, and in other languages they obviously are. This state of affairs is not universal in any language system however, since languages have to be flexible in order to work at all. So specific or original meanings of words are generalised or extended, usually on the basis of some similarity or association between the things being denoted. A benign example is the word ride, originally denoting the activity of riding a horse, and then extended to *ride a bicycle*, *ride (on) a train*, *ride a storm*, etc. There is a kind of metaphorical comparison between the activities involved, and at the same time an extension of the set of words which *ride* goes with. The extended senses of *ride* are said to be 'motivated': i.e. it is not just 'arbitrary' that we say 'ride' a bike or 'ride' a storm, though it would have been if we had invented a separate word for the separate activity (like 'sprobe a bike', 'bleek a storm'). Many compound words have obvious motivation: *typewriter* (instead of an arbitrary new word like 'sprontobe'). Motivation is a kind of recursive process in which language preys on itself in order to yield something – a meaning – which is the same but different. Obviously, the learning and use of new words is facilitated if they are motivated. Notice also that the system provides wide margins of choice for which items are motivated in which ways, and this leaves scope for manipulation, if (as is the case in some subvarieties) extensions of meaning are engineered by groups with specific interests.

Now much of nukespeak can be regarded as the product of the motivation or remotivation of existing language resources. This malignant process can be illustrated (and will be in later sections) on many levels. On the level of individual words, *warhead* (like *typewriter*) would be an example of a motivated rather than an arbitrary string of words. Examples of the extension of original meanings and of collocations are the words *war* and *peace* themselves. *Cold* is (was?) an unlikely collocate of *war*; the term *war* in *cold war* seems to refer to a state of affairs that is not really *war* in its usual (old?) sense. Similarly, *peace* has had its meaning changed (you might say perverted). *Missile* (and *gun*, *bomb*, etc) would collocate with *war*. Its range has been extended to collocate with *peace*, as in 'missiles of peace' (a phrase used by John Nott). *Pacifist* can be a term of abuse. Michael Foot's *peacemonger* is an interesting counter shot, thought it too is abusive when used in a pro-nuclear context.[9] And Reagan's 'peacekeeper' (cognomen of the MX missile, preferred to the originally proposed 'peacemaker') only makes sense if referred to a whole ideology of cold war and deterrence.

It is, however, above all on the level of phrases that the existing language can be remotivated to yield categorisations of reality that are in the interests of specific ideologies. This is made easy because technical and scientific language, the prestige language of the nuclear age, frequently uses complex noun phrases for precision, made up of combinations of adjectives and, more imposingly, nouns qualifying the head noun. The effect is to make relatively perspicuous a system of classification and subclassification that would be obscured if arbitrary new terms were coined. The naming of chemical compounds is a case in point; here the system is well-constrained and has obvious utility in the interests of the communication of knowledge, at least within the scientific community. This practice is aped by would-be scientific 'experts' of many kinds, and nuclear policy is the most dangerous case. A clear and relatively simple example is the way in which weapons have been categorised. The things exist in the real world, but the way they are mentally categorised and typecast is not a function of the objects themselves, but of the minds of their makers and users. The vocabulary consumed by the general public increases and becomes slightly larger, but it places a crude simplifying grid over the complex technological reality and its implications. The first semantic extension affected *bomb*. After 1945 bombs had to be reclassified into *bombs* and *atomic bombs*, and subsequently into *bombs*, *atomic-bombs* and *hydrogen-bombs*:

$$
\left\{
\begin{array}{l}
bomb \\
\\
atomic\ bomb
\end{array}
\right.
\qquad
\left\{
\begin{array}{l}
bomb \\
atomic\ bomb \\
hydrogen\ bomb
\end{array}
\right.
$$

The term 'bomb' is significantly altered in this process. Before extension, it was linked in all probability in people's minds with a collective myth of the survival of the blitz, with a specific idea as to the limits of their destructiveness, and with a specific idea as to their survivability. These ideas associated with the word, at least for a certain generation of speakers, are now quite irrelevant. With the increased sophistication of 'delivery systems' (a nukespeak term for aircraft, missiles – itself an extension of the older meaning of 'a thing that can be thrown to do damage' – guns, surface ships and submarines, which itself represents another example of the reorganisation of semantic space), the term 'bomb' was no longer appropriate, and was replaced by the generic term *weapon*. At least 'bomb' was concrete and specific. 'Weapon' includes *any* implement that can inflict damage. Even the qualified 'nuclear weapon' can be misleading, as Paul Rogers points out, because it seems to want to refer only to the nuclear 'device' (more nukespeak), not to the rocket, gun or aircraft which projects it, and because it consequently gives little indication of the potential of the whole contraption.[10]. More important, however, is the subclassification of nuclear weapons, which I tentatively represent below:

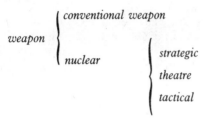

There are of course other words in use, but this system is perhaps the most impressive and the most insidious. It does not correspond to anything like the variety of nuclear weapons actually in existence. It confuses technical specification ('nuclear') with possible function ('tactical', etc.). It creates the impression that there are discrete physical categories of weapon, and that the use of each type can be contained. A noun phrase like *theatre nuclear weapon* thus classifies and subclassifies *weapons*, and creates an entity of highly dubious status.

These examples illustrate ways in which existing vocabulary items can have their meaning extended to new objects, processes, experiences, etc. Both *bomb* and *weapon* now refer to things significantly different from the things they referred to thirty or forty years ago. It is possible that there are differences between generations in the way the terms are understood. And it may also be possible that the semantic space of these and other terms in nukespeak is too extended (in the sense that they include in their reference objects of quite different orders of destructiveness) for our safety.

In the extension process some sort of analogy seems to be at work. The greater the 'distance' between the two domains involved in the analogy, the closer we are to metaphor: *ride a horse, ride a bicycle, ride a storm; bomb, atomic bomb, go (like) a bomb.* Analogy and metaphor in various guises are extremely productive processes of nukespeak, because analogies can be chosen to change the way people see things. Everything from the construction of impressive nicknames for weapons to the construction of extended quasi-logical arguments can be based on analogy and metaphor. The term *theatre* above is an example (though less potent perhaps than some we shall see later) of a kind of metaphorical extension. From its original sense (space for acting, hence action) it was long ago extended to its sense of a locus of military operations. In nukespeak it is extended a bit further by being used as a classifier of weapon types, and by being used as an adjective could be used (notice that one cannot talk of 'theatrical nuclear weapons'!). It is impossible to say to what extent the original 'theatre' metaphor is still functional here. For the strategists who coined it, amongst others, it is probably not functional; but it would be rash to assume that it does not conjure up some strange images for some speakers in the population.

I have given special attention to aspects of semantic change – or semantic hijacking as it might more aptly be called in the present context.[11] It is not the only aspect of nukespeak, though it is perhaps the most important because it concerns vocabulary that is actively produced by a group of speakers; moreover, it is not just passively heard by people whose thoughts and attitudes may or may not be modified; it is actually *used* by them in conversation and discussion. In addition, however, one has to take into account various other devices of linguistic persuasion used by the pro-nuclear apologists. These are devices based on choice of vocabulary, grammatical constructions, rhetorical patterning – and let us here include clichés, catch-phrases and slogans – which are not necessarily confined to the subject of nuclear arms, but are common in all coercive speakers, from politicians to preachers. The pressure on speakers in the population at large to use such tricks is clearly far less than in the case of specialised vocabulary. They are none the less important, since those on the receiving end may be impressed and even convinced by them.

I have been trying to show some of the ways in which the arbitrary units of language can be taken and reformed into motivated chunks which can be put into circulation and swallowed whole. We can return at this point to our first set of questions and ask 'motivated by whom'? If words and phrases are (in Bollinger's words) just *there* for our use, who put them there? Until relatively recently linguists have talked about languages as if they were undifferentiated, homogeneous units. A fairly widespread view of how people come to be able to communicate with one another through language at all is that languages are tacit conventions between members of the speech community as a whole. In other words there is a kind of consensus as to which syntactic structures, which items of vocabulary, shall 'count' for purposes of communication. But this surely cannot always be true, and is probably true less often than one would like to think. At the very least, convention must mean a dynamic jostling for competing forms of language. But even this view overlooks cases where languages or forms of a language are actually imposed by force or otherwise on populations or sections of populations. The limiting case is the imposition of a foreign language on a conquered population. (The speaking of Gaelic in Scotland used to be illegal.) Nonstandard social and geographical dialects of a national language may also be a source of conflict, with their speakers being stigmatised and disadvantaged. Sections of the speech community may even, as part of their emancipation, come to find the particular structure of the national language unacceptable. This is the case with those portions of vocabulary and grammar relating to sexual differences and sexual dominance which feminists have found to be loaded against them.

I want to propose that something similar is the case for nukespeak. Existing language is processed, subjected to numerous semantic readjustments, and fed back to the population predominantly via the media. People then consume it – that is, use it to exchange meanings among themselves – not because they are intrinsically incapable of seeing through it and creating alternative means of expression, but because it is easier and simpler to make use of what is to hand. In addition, there are subtle pressures to comply in the form of stigmatisation of people who don't master prestige technical jargon, and even in the form of explicit demands that if you want to argue with the strategists you should use the language of the strategists. Anyone who wants to bypass the language game set up against them will have some difficulty in doing so. A simplified and highly hypothetical model of the nukespeak network is given below:

A Nukespeak Network

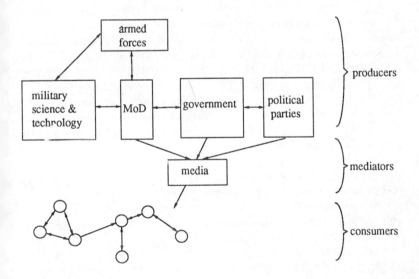

The direction of the arrowheads is meant to indicate the predominant direction of communication. I assume that some organs do not, or are unable to, respond or provide feedback. In other words, some people talk to one another, and some are talked to or talked at. The producers of nukespeak talk to one another, and the consumers of nukespeak talk to one another, but the two groups on the whole do *not* intercommunicate. What happens is that the producers produce the basic vocabulary of nukespeak and numerous linguistically packaged arguments, which are assimilated to varying degrees by the consumers. The media are the distributors of the nukespeak commodity. It is well known that by and large their information on defence matters derives from Ministry of Defence press officers and judicious official 'leaks', and that in addition dependencies between media, political and commercial institutions can act as effective filters and censors. At the receiving end, people do not have the possibility of response, and are liable to regard what they see on television and read in the papers as objective and unbiased. Of course this picture is an oversimplification: in reality, the boxes are not watertight; the boundaries are fuzzy and there are individuals who overstep them. The picture is merely intended as a hypothesis about the *predominant* directions of influence.

Like advertising, propaganda in Western democracies has to sell a product. In the case of fall-out shelters, indeed, propaganda and advertising seem to be identical. Deterrents (like detergents) have to be sold. Taxpayers buy weapons in the sense that they choose the governments who buy them (though in terms of defence policies the choice has not been too broad). There is no question of buying or selling if governments spend your money without telling you (as in the case of the Chevaline development and the Trident decision), but if the arms race is 'democratised' (that is, if certain facts about Cruise, Pershing and Trident are noised abroad), then specific propaganda becomes necessary: recent years have seen good examples of this. The problem facing the propagandists is then very like that facing cigarette advertisers. Once large numbers of people come to believe that cigarettes (like nuclear missiles) can damage your health, advertisers have to work very hard to modify, eliminate or repress that belief. Thus when the idea got around that Cruise missiles could be a danger to local populations, government propaganda tried to convince people that not only were they really a form of protection, but that they were also 'safe'.

The most general point that can be made about the processes of nukespeak is probably this: it is a stretching of existing language to tame, familiarise and naturalise inventions and experiences of unprecented historical significance. This taming, however, is not entirely due to people in general, but largely and increasingly due to interested manipulation of language.

6

Revealing Metaphors

This chapter is, in part, about bears, baseball, giants, pumpkins and priests...if that sounds like a fairy story, then actually the idea of a *story* is also going to to be relevant to what I want to say. But beside the idea of *story* (or *script* or *frame* or *schema*, which is the terminology we'll be using), I want to give a good deal of attention to the concept of *metaphor* and its role. in the organisation or understanding of public discourse: which is where the bears, giants and the rest come in...More specifically, I want to look at the way this kind of metaphor operates in discourse about things nuclear, and my general aim will be to build up a framework for analysing the use of metaphors in political discourse of all kinds.

There are two main concepts, then:

1) story (or frame, or script, or schema); and
2) metaphor; and to this I should add a third thing which I shall tentatively call a
3) metaphor – morphism.

The idea of 'frame' first emerged in the attempts to stimulate human cognition and perception on computers. The basic problem can be seen from an example given by Minsky, the originator of frame theory:

> Just before you enter a room, you usually know enough to 'expect' a room rather than, say, a landscape. You can usually tell just by the character of the door. And you can often select in advance a frame for the new room.[1]

What this implies is that people store knowledge about different kinds of rooms and what they look like, i.e. they have *expectations* which will operate by *default* until modified by contrary information. In the case of rooms, to quote Minsky again,

> A typical room-frame has three visible walls, each perhaps of a different 'kind'. One knows many kinds of walls: walls with windows, shelves, pictures, and fireplaces. Each room has its own kind of walls, etc.etc.[2]

To represent this in a computer program is a complicated business – but to do so also gives an insight into the complicated way human minds work.

Let us extend the application of the *frame* idea further to another famous example developed by Schank and Abelson and others: the 'restaurant *script*' or 'story'.[3] Abelson argues that 'scripts' are structured collections of knowledge, often socially based, concerning stereotype situations (that is, frequently recurring ones) such as visits to restaurants, birthday parties, train journeys, cricket matches, seeing tutors about essays...the list has no set limits, and you might like to think up your own examples. To convince us of the existence of 'scripts', Abelson asks us to consider two stories, one of which has coherence and connectivity between its constituent sentences, one of which doesn't:

a)   John went to a restaurant. He asked the waitress for *coq au vin*.
b)   John went to a park. He asked the midget for a mouse. He picked up the box and left.

Abelson's point is that in (b) 'We are unprepared for the reference to "the" midget rather than "a" midget, and "the" box rather than "a" box. Furthermore, we are incapable of connecting the last two lines of the story, without a great deal of effort'.[4] The fact that we react differently to the two 'stories' is, he claims, due to the fact that we have a restaurant script stored in memory, but not a standard mouse-midget-and-box script. To put it slightly differently, the-midget-and-the-mouse story is a *new* story, visiting restaurants is an *old* story – rather in the same way as the tale of Little Red Riding Hood is an *old* story with a script you know, so that it is not at all surprising if I say '...and as she went through the wood, she met *the* wolf...' (rather than 'she met a wolf').

What, you may be asking at this point, does all this have to do with the discourse of nuclear politics and nuclear weapons? The answer, briefly, is that we can take the idea of *scripts* (or 'frames') one step further, and propose that the political beliefs, assumptions and expectations that people hold are a bit like scripts. That is to say, just as people have assumptions about what happens in restaurants (what roles the various participants play), so people have assumptions about, for example, the roles played by Americans, Russians, Communists, Capitalists, etc. In fact, Abelson developed what he called a 'Cold War Script' and the idea was taken up in work by William Downes.[5]

It is not essential here to concern ourselves too closely with the nuts and bolts of Abelson's actual programme design (his ideas of conceptual 'atoms', 'molecules', etc.); but there are two main general points that are full of implications for the preoccupations of the present book. The first is philosophical. Can computers really think like people? Can Abelson's so-called 'Ideology Machine' really tell us about the way people handle ideological beliefs? This is, of course, a far-reaching question that is hotly disputed at the moment by philosophers and computer scientists,. and all I want to do is throw out the following idea. Maybe it is true that computers can never really think, never really *mean* anything in an intentional sense (as Searle argued). But suppose we turn the question round: Do humans sometimes 'think' like computers? Put like this, the question looks rather different. Perhaps indeed people *do* – or some people under some circumstances do – 'think' like machines: such a case would indeed be the cold-war ideology machine described by Abelson. We all know the kind of political ideologue who has knee-jerk reflexes when asked if the Soviets are a threat, what he or she thinks about CND or the freeze movement, striking miners, striking railwaymen...and so on. This way of stating the question is in tune with Orwell's notion of mechanical speech, though the computer analogy is far from his universe of thought. There are more ramifications to thought, and artificial intelligence, than can be adequately handled here, so I shall go on to my second main point about Abelson's 'Ideology Machine', which will bring us to the main topic of this chapter. The second point, then, is this: that Abelson's framework for the workings of his 'Ideology Machine' is only a small part of the story. His essential ingredients are: stereotype actors (Communists, Liberals, Free World) and stereotypical actions and attributes associated with them (schemes to dominate the world, fuzzy thinking, 'wet' or 'soft' ideas, 'naivety', 'aggressiveness', 'love of peace'; it is easy to extend the list from one's internalised knowledge of this kind of discourse). The thing that distinguishes an ideological script from, say, a restaurant script is the fact than an ideological script does not *necessarily* correspond to real roles, actions and properties in the real world. So there has to be some additional support, motivation or justification for the basic output of the ideology machine. Abelson himself hints at this:

> Many ideological, nationalistic and/or idealistic scripts postulate dra-matic theme ... transitions supported by flimsy metaphors or evanescent motivational constructs. 'The War to End All Wars', 'The Domino Theory', and 'The Withering away of the State' are three such exam-ples. (Abelson 1973: p. 326).

We might return to these examples, but to see the kind of thing I am getting at, consider the following:

...with a single-party state, with the Soviet leadership in the possession of overwhelming and still growing military power, *who can be certain* of the future? *Who can tell* what problems will come for its successors, with popular discontent inevitable over living standards, with demographic problems ... and all this held together by a repressive bureaucracy and supplied by a heavily over-centralized and inefficient economic system? *Can we disregard* totally even the possibility in years to come of a disintegrating Soviet empire, with, as an act of desperation, the dying giant lashing out across the central front? (speech in the House of Commons by the then Foreign Secretary, John Nott, 7 July 1981)

In order to comprehend the processes of thought that give rise to texts of this type, we can ask questions like the following:

– What claims about the Soviet Union's *intentions* is Nott making?
– *How* does he back up his claim, make it convincing as an account of political reality?
– What's the 'flimsy metaphor' that Abelson mentions as supporting such scripts?

What Nott wants to do, it seems, is to assert the likelihood of Russia attacking Europe. To 'prove' this (and I use the word *'prove'* advisedly, as we shall see), what he does is to assert certain features of the Soviet Union – the bureaucracy, the military, the single party, etc. – which are facts beyond reasonable dispute. But how does he get from here to 'proving' that the Soviet Union will, *as a necessary consequence* of these things, invade the West? Partly he does it by rhetorical questions (which invite the hearer to accept the speaker's presuppositions) but, crucially, what he does is use a *metaphor*.

What does this metaphor assert? It asserts that the Soviet Union is a *giant*. Now, there is a *script* for giant stories which we've all been reared on: giants are nasty and aggressive; they eat innocent children; when they die, they lash out in a wild frenzy; but giants are also often overcome by small but heroic mortals called Jack or David.[7]

So here the *metaphor* may be playing an important role in structuring the way we understand the political reality of the Soviet Union and our relationship with it. And *the concept of metaphor* is what I now want to explore before going on to further examples and ideas.

Let us try to set up a useful definition of metaphor. Most people would probably say that metaphor involved using a word non-literally, or applying a word to an object to which it was not literally applicable.

This gives the impression that metaphors don't really matter, that they're not 'meant' seriously, that they're only stylistic ornaments, and so forth. Whether or not that is the way the man or woman-in-the-street thinks of metaphor, if they think of it at all, the fact is that all people surely use metaphor (certainly they hear and interpret metaphor) every day of their lives. So it is reasonable to enquire what metaphor is doing *to* them or *for* them – what is metaphor for? (Incidentally, if metaphor *is* actually a force exerting real influence on discourse yet at the same time considered trivial or unimportant, think how useful it is for Mr Nott and others to be able to back off and say 'Oh, it's only metaphor, you know!').

Now when you look at accounts of metaphor from the early days of Greek rhetoric onward, you find that it has often been taken very seriously indeed. There is a vast literature, in fact, on the subject, and we can (and need) only pick out a few points that might serve our present purposes.

Aristotle, for instance, in his *Poetics* and *Rhetoric* clearly regards metaphor in cognitive terms: it is part of the process of making sense of reality. In particular, it enables us to get hold of new ideas:

> Strange words simply puzzle us; ordinary words convey only what we know already; it is from metaphor that we can best get hold of something fresh.[8]

And the way this getting hold of new ideas worked was by the perception of resemblances. These two ideas – perception of resemblance and the grasping of new ideas – give us a clue to the role of metaphor in nuclear discourse (and, of course, in other discourses) in the post-1945 world. Atomic energy and atomic explosions were not only frightening in themselves, they were frightening because the physics involved, and the extraordinary complexity of the scientific aspects, were and are difficult for most minds to conceive. Metaphors and analogies aimed at explaining nuclear mysteries abounded in the popular press in the 1940s and 1950s. Equally, the complexities of the behaviour of nation-states on the international scene is beyond ordinary comprehension and prediction: here too the role of metaphor is crucial, as the Nott text and others suggest.

If we look for another landmark in the history of the concept of metaphor, we find an interesting development in Renaissance Europe, in the work of Petrus Ramus (1515–72), a philosopher and rhetorician of tremendous influence, who, to put it crudely, broke down the ancient division between *logic* on the one hand and *rhetoric* on the other. The result is interesting – metaphors can now be thought of as part of the process of logical thought, i.e. a means of reasoning and arriving at valid conclusions. One consequence of the Ramist view of metaphor – that metaphors themselves are logical arguments – is that metaphor is *not* a special device confined to literature, as the classical tradition had come to suggest, and as the present-day school tradition gives pupils to believe.

If metaphor is not just a bit of poetic fancy limited to the literary ghetto, just what is its scope and significance? Probably the most important recent discussion of this topic is to be found in Lakoff and Johnson's *Metaphors We Live By*.[9] The fundamental point is that metaphor is not just a matter of *words*, let alone just a matter of literature: 'Metaphor is pervasive in everyday life, not just in language but in thought and action. Our ordinary conceptual system, in terms of which we both think and act, is fundamentally metaphorical in nature' (p. 3). It is a matter, as Aristotle argued, of resemblances and of perception, in fact of perceiving one thing in terms of another. Indeed, we may want to add, it is a question of perceiving one thing or *script* (*frame*) in terms of another *script* (*frame*).

Now, armed (to use a metaphor) with their definition of metaphor, we need to consider just which bits of utterances we shall count as metaphors. Traditional pedagogy distinguishes between 'dead' and 'live' metaphor. Instead of a dichotomy, however, it is probably useful to think in terms of different degrees of *metaphorical penetration*.

What I mean by this, quite simply, is that some metaphorical structures are more firmly entrenched (and thus less noticed) in our language, perhaps all languages, than others. That is, at a fundamental level some metaphorical structures seem to be a natural and quite indispensable part of our semantic system, of the way we think and express ourselves. For example, it has recently been argued (Jackendoff, 1983) that all events and states in our conceptual/semantic structure 'are organised according to a very limited set of principles, drawn primarily from the conceptualization of space'. Thus *time* is in English (and, as Whorf pointed out, in other Indo-European languages) encoded linguistically in terms of *space*: e.g. we say 'at 11.00' and 'at the polytechnic', 'in 1985' and 'in the box', 'from Monday to Wednesday' and 'from Coventry to Cardiff', and so on. This can be extended to verbs: e.g. 'my lecture went/extended/ran from 3.00 to 5.00 without *stopping*', 'the road went/extended/ran from Birmingham to Bristol'. This type of analysis can be widely extended throughout the semantic system. If metaphorical transfer in this sense is so basic a part of our conceptual apparatus, then it's not surprising to find it occurring at other levels of language and language use.

At a second level of stability one finds the so-called 'dead metaphors' or 'idioms' which have become a part of what seems natural in our language but which are quite likely to be culture-specific rather than a universal aspect of human cognition. Lakoff and Johnson discuss, for instance, cases such as the following:

Your claims are indefensible
He attacked every weak point in my argument
His criticisms were right on target
I demolished her argument
I've never won an argument with her
His rhetoric was devastating

In all such cases we can ask: what is being seen in terms of what? And here, Lakoff and Johnson claim, the proposition all such sentences point to is: *argument is war*.

This, then, is a relatively permanent metaphor in English and other languages: it is presumably a product of certain cultural forms, certain ways of conducting our affairs in social life. As to whether the existence of these metaphors in turn reinforces, influences or even determines the way people conceive their culture and relationships – that is an open question. But there is little doubt that such metaphors are productive – that is, lexically and syntactically novel utterances will reflect the same underlying proposition.

At the third level, on this very rough scale of 'metaphorical penetration', are metaphors which, while being in various ways a product of our cultural symbols, do come and go according to the interests of particular people in particular places at particular times. As we shall see in more detail below, one particular property of metaphor is highly useful for anyone seeking to plant a particular picture of reality in people's minds – the property of *entailments*. The best way to explain this is again to quote Lakoff and Johnson:

> For example, faced with the energy crisis, President Carter declared it 'the moral equivalent of war.' The *war* metaphor generated a network of entailments. There was an 'enemy', a 'threat to national security', which required 'setting targets', 'reorganizing priorities', 'establishing a new chain of command', 'plotting new strategy', 'gathering intelligence', 'marshalling forces', 'imposing sanctions', 'calling for sacrifices', and on and on. The metaphor was not merely a way of viewing reality; it con-stituted a license for policy change and political and economic action...it is important to realise that this was not the only metaphor available.[10].

This last point is indeed an important one. Suppose, for instance, Mr Nott had not chosen to assume that *the Soviet Union is a giant* and activate his giant script? Even more important, he needn't have used a *metaphor* at all: in seeking to make sense of historical processes, metaphor may not be in any sense a valid way of reasoning. But the whole question of whether a particular metaphor is a valid one brings us to the notion of *morphisms* – indeed to *pumpkins* and *baseball*.

For the *pumpkin* and *baseball* metaphor, consider the following:

> (1) We insist on serving up these veto pitches that come over the plate the size of a pumpkin. (Democratic Congressman complaining about the President's easy vetoing of controversial bills, quoted in *Newsweek*, 7 July 1975.)

The reason for quoting this is not just that it comes from the political domain, but because it comes from a research paper by an artificial intelligence researcher[11] who brings together the two notions we've been looking at – viz. *scripts* (or 'frames', or 'schemas') and *metaphor* – precisely in order to make computationally explicit the role of both these things in processes of thought. I shall therefore try to summarise briefly his proposals – but add two slightly different slants of my own, namely (1) the idea of morphism, which comes from mathematics, but is a fairly elementary aspect of mathematical reasoning, and (2) the suggestion that metaphorical reasoning is particularly prevalent in the kind of 'ideology machine' described in the 1970s by Abelson.

Hobbs, then, starts from the kind of view of metaphor I've already outlined: that is, he assumes that in constructing a computer-applicable text-understanding system, it will be necessary to take account of metaphor in 'ordinary language' to start with. For example, he points out that spatial metaphors are pervasive in, for example, even the abstract reasoning of mathematics: e.g. N is *at* zero, N *goes from* 1 *to* 100, etc.

Then he comes to pumpkins and baseball, which he takes to be a 'novel metaphor'. There are actually *two* metaphors here, and the primary one is *baseball*. In Lakoff and Johnson's terms, there is an underlying proposition which says something like *Congress is a baseball game*. Whether that is strictly *novel* is debatable: as I suggested earlier, such metaphors are quite likely to be products of cultural forms and in this case there is a cluster of metaphors which relate perhaps to the *argument is war* metaphor. After all, *politics is argument* in Western democracies; moreover, *war is a game* and *vice versa*. So *politics is a game* and *Congress is a baseball game* are not surprising conclusions. Be that as it may, what concerns Hobbs is to show 'how metaphorical reasoning works'. According to him, it works like this: there is a baseball schema ('script', 'frame') with certain roles and actions and a 'congressional bill schema' with its roles and actions, and the two schema can be matched up thus:

Congress	*pitcher*
bill	*ball*
President	*batter*
send	*pitch*
sign	*miss*
veto	*hit*

Hobbs's claim is that in order to produce or understand argument (1) above we have to bring these two 'frames' into correspondence (although there are obviously additional complexities). He makes a further point which is highly relevant to the use of metaphor in political contexts. The point is that many inferences can be drawn from the metaphorical schema (i.e. the baseball schema here); some of these are liable to be transferred back to the Congress-President schema, while others aren't. For instance, the ball itself is spherical and has stitching, but it makes no sense to relate this to the corresponding literal item, the Bill. On the other hand, there *is* a clear suggestion, to quote Hobbs, 'that Congress and President are adversaries in the same way that a pitcher and a batter are, and that from the President's perspective it is good for him to veto a bill Congress has passed and bad for him to sign it.'[12] (It *may*, of course, be true that Congress and President are adversaries, but such actual correspondence is not *necessarily* the case for all metaphors.)

Now Hobbs generalises from this example to give us a useful framework we can think of in terms of a mathematical morphism, which brings us back in a curious way to Aristotle's idea that metaphor's function is to enable us to grasp fresh ideas. Without getting too mathematical, a morphism exists when you can prove or calculate something by mapping one set of things into another, doing the proof or calculation in another domain, and then mapping back to the problematic domain you were first interested in. Logarithms work a bit like this:

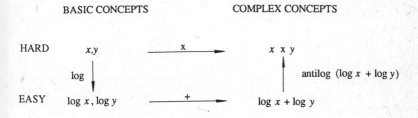

Corresponding to the mathematical symbols and functions, Hobbs's account suggests, we see certain kinds of natural thought processes in terms of basic concepts, complex structures of concepts, and metaphorical mappings between domains. The general idea is that if you have a difficult or uncertain domain – like Congress (or for that matter the super power conflict) – and want to draw conclusions about it, one way you can do this is to construct what we might call a *metaphor morphism*; that is to say, you transfer the basic term of the problematic domain into the terms of some domain which has a more familiar schema (e.g. giants for Mr Nott, bears and bulldogs, baseball games, etc), then you draw some relevant deduction (e.g. giants lash out when they die, bulldogs stand up to wild animals, batters bash balls, etc) and translate the deduction back to the first, 'literal', domain of primary concern: e.g. the Soviet Union will attack the West, the President opposes Congress, etc.

The only snag is this: you cannot always make valid morphisms in mathematics, and equally you should not assume that all metaphorical analogies are valid in ordinary language. It is not just a matter of whether a metaphor is aesthetically pleasing or not; it's a matter of whether it will be conceptually misleading, whether it will lead to a potentially dangerous interpretation of reality.

To conclude, let us look at some further examples of nuclear discourse which employs a metaphorical mode of reasoning. The following passage is a Ministry of Defence pamphlet intended to persuade people of the necessity to increase British nuclear weapons systems:

HOW TO DEAL WITH A BULLY

PEACE THROUGH DETERRENCE – THE ONLY ANSWER TO A BULLY'S THREAT

Many of us have had to stand up to a bully at some stage in our lives. The only answer is to say: 'Let me alone – or you'll be sorry.' And to have the strength to back up your words.

The situation is just the same between Russia and the West. Britain and NATO must have the strength to face up to the threat of Soviet military might. And that means Britain and NATO must have nuclear weapons.

Here the problematic domain includes the Soviet Union and UK nuclear weapons. The known domain includes the bully script, which says something like: 'Bullies always attack weaker victims: the only way *not* to be attacked is to look strong.' Thus we can outline a metaphor morphism as follows:

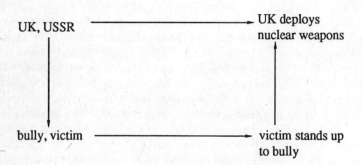

In this case, then, the *need* for nuclear weapons is deduced from a claim that international relations can be conceptualised in terms of the school playground; as you can see, the analogy is made very explicit. One key advantage (to the speaker) is that the bully script (like

baseball) is taken for granted – it's assumed to be part of nature and so the Soviet Union is assumed to be an aggressive threat. The power of the metaphor lies also· in the fact that it is not easy – though it's certainly not impossible – to question such presuppositions. There is also a second, parallel, metaphor here based on the illustration of the bulldog and the bear which adorns the front of the folded pamphlet. The same kind of conceptualisation and reasoning can clearly be conveyed in a non-linguistic mode, though this mode is here obviously interacting with the verbal metaphor.

This type of analysis reveals a kind of para-logic only tenuously related to the practical, empirical rationality often claimed by texts in the political arena. It can also reveal the stability and influence of certain metaphors in texts of different types and dates. Consider, for instance, the following:

In 1972, Alvin Weinberg, director of the Oak Ridge National Laboratory from 1955 to 1973, wrote an article in the journal *Science* in which he suggested that a *technological 'priesthood'* might be necessary to ensure that nuclear power was managed properly in perpetuity. Weinberg argued that nuclear technology is a particular demanding technology, and that society might need to evolve new social institutions to handle it. The development of nuclear weapons, he wrote, 'in a sense...established a *military priesthood* which guards against inadvertent use of nuclear weapons....[13]

Each country now has its own AEC that sets standards or, in some cases, actually monitors or operates reactors. Perhaps this will be sufficient for ever. Yet no government has lasted continuously for 1,000 years: only the *Catholic Church* has survived more or less continuously for 2,000 years or so. Our commitment to nuclear energy is assumed to last in perpetuity – can we think of a national entity that possesses the resiliency to remain. alive for even a single half-life of plutonium-239? A permanent cadre of experts that will retain its continuity over immensely long times hardly seems feasible if the cadre is a national body.

It may be that an International Authority, operating as an agent of the United Nations, could become the focus for this cadre of expertise. The experts themselves would remain under national auspices, but they would be part of a worldwide community of experts who are held together, are monitored, and are given long-term stability by the International Authority. The *Catholic Church* is the best example of what I have in mind: a central authority that *proclaims* and to a degree enforces *doctrine*, maintains its own long-term social stability, and has connections to every country's own Catholic Church.[14]

It seems that the dangers of handling plutonium were not at the time fully realised and the risk of contamination at the plant was high. Dr Donald Geesaman, a nuclear physicist who visited the plant, later commented: 'We had been led to believe that, somehow, in the nuclear age, accidents would be impossible because everything would be handled by a nuclear priesthood, who would be so absolute in their perfection that they would be able to handle this unforgiving fuel cycle. Then you go down to Oklahoma and what do you find? A bunch of high-school kids ... It's mind boggling.'[15]

Following the methods we have already discussed, we might clarify the structures of thought employed in these texts by means of the following metaphor morphism:

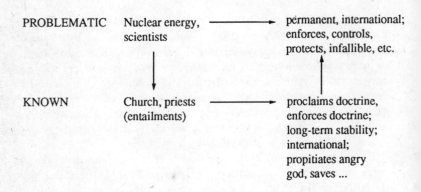

PROBLEMATIC	Nuclear energy, scientists	permanent, international; enforces, controls, protects, infallible, etc.
KNOWN	Church, priests (entailments)	proclaims doctrine, enforces doctrine; long-term stability; international; propitiates angry god, saves ...

An interesting feature in these particular texts is that metaphorical reasoning is used not to restructure an already existing set of ideas but as a blueprint for concrete action. A second point is that the metaphor was clearly not an isolated rhetorical flight of fancy – it had got planted in the minds of the scientific community and various inferences, apparently unconscious, had begun to sprout spontaneously, as Dr Geesaman's surprise strongly suggests. In fact, the ease with which powerful metaphors can be got into circulation via the media is quite remarkable. A further and final example is the passage reproduced below, which shows the evolution of a particularly powerful metaphor that dominated Japanese nuclear discourse in the mid-1960s:

In the background seems to be the U.S. government's desire for the Japanese to put greater trust in the U.S., expecting that, if enough time goes by, Japan's 'nuclear weapons allergy' will be eliminated

(*Asahi Shimbun*, 29 August 1964).

The United States, as the user of bases in Japan, should not merely call this kind of feeling [popular opposition to the call of a US nuclear-weapon loaded aircraft carrier] among the Japanese people a nuclear allergy, and such like, and make light of it (*Asahi Shimbun*, 28 October 1966).

...the question of nuclear allergy has been raised. I think it is necessary to eliminate this, the nuclear allergy. I think it can be said to be the result of not having a correct understanding of [nuclear matters]. If there were correct understanding then there would be no nuclear allergy. Again, in regard to peaceful use and so on, I think there ought to be a higher appreciation of nuclear power...(Prime Minister Sato on the return of the *Okinawa* with or without nuclear weapons, 22 December 1967).[16]

The allergy metaphor, which is related to more general cultural metaphors of health and disease, and of the state as a body (the body politic), has particularly far-reaching implications. Associated with the idea of allergy is a script or frame of assumptions something like this:

- allergens are substances harmless to normal people
- abnormally sensitive people can be desensitised by exposure
- doctors can cure the allergy by gradual desensitisation, i.e. by increased doses of the allergen.

When this frame is mapped onto the nuclear domain, you get interesting inferences:

- nuclear weapons etc. are harmless to normal people
- people who dislike them are abnormally sensitive and need to be 'cured'
- the Japanese people were sensitised by the atomic bombing of Hiroshima and Nagasaki and need to be desensitised, by increasing their contact with nuclear weapons installations (i.e. by means of visits by US warships, government propaganda, and so on).

It also follows that the politicians seeking to 'eliminate the allergy' are cast in the role of doctors.

The point is that the metaphorical domain is taken for granted and familiar, and is used to structure a problematic reality. And again, once the metaphor is well established, it is not that easy for it to be challenged. There are considerable risks in the deep rooted habit of metaphorical thinking. Let us conclude by recalling some relevant remarks by two thinkers from very different scientific backgrounds. One is Einstein, who pointed out that 'the power set free from the atom has changed everything, except our ways of thought', and that if we are to survive 'we must learn to think in a new way'.[17] And the other is the linguist, anthropologist and fire insurance inspector Benjamin Lee Whorf, who argued that our ways of thinking were inextricably bound up with our ways of talking. One thing that worried him as a linguist and safety inspector was that petrol drums that were full of flammable gas were labelled *empty*; people were continually dropping cigarette ends in them. It may be worth considering this in metaphorical relation to a world full of nuclear warheads labelled 'for security'.

War, Work and

Falklands Talk

In the early summer of 1982, well-primed Conservative MPs visited their constituencies explaining to the faithful how the Falklands episode not only regenerated and united the nation, but also how it was part and parcel of our role in the new cold war. They (and not only they) adopted at that time a set of rhetorical arguments and other propaganda devices which show a marked militarisation of certain areas of political discourse. One MP at least (Iain Mills, member for Meriden) has spoken with pride of a future *militarist* government. Maybe there's more than chance similarity in sound with the word *monetarist*. But the main point is that here is a significant shift in usage. Words ending in *-ist* and *-ism* normally have a habit of becoming pejorative – a tendency that makes them markers of the ideological divisions of our culture. For large numbers of people, *pacifism*, *communism*, *conservatism*, etc., are sneer words, although for equally large numbers they are cheer words. Yet until recently few people would have used *militarist* in anything other than a pejorative sense. After all, we were agreed that the *militarist* regime in Argentina was a bad thing. It is interesting, therefore, to see it being used by a politician about something he manifestly considers a *good* thing.

In 1982 Conservative talk on defence set the Falklands war in the context of the new cold war propaganda as purveyed by what the Ministry of Defence called 'Spring offensive against the Campaign for Nuclear Disarmament'. In effect, this is instant history, constructed in the interests of those who construct it. In some of these accounts of the history of the Falklands the original claim that 'we' were standing up to the Argentines has been obscured by the claim that the war was necessary to show 'our' muscle to the Soviets. This even includes the claim that, had *strength* and *resolution* and the rest not been shown, then the Russians would have been encouraged to invade the United Kingdom and to take over our oil and coal reserves. It seems incredible that anyone should take this seriously. But it can still be effective as propaganda, even if it is not taken *literally*. The way I have heard it used, it is presented rhetorically and hyperbolically. In any use, it is a purely hypothetical statement with no basis in historical fact. Whether the audience takes it or leaves it as a truth claim, the notion of The Threat is none the less powerfully insinuated. This technique – evading the responsibility of making explicit statements and leading the hearer to draw his or her own conclusions – is common enough in all types of propaganda. 'Do They Really Want Peace?' asked a current Tory poster. Don't say who 'They' are, though 'They' are clearly not Us, but the Other, the Alien. And don't answer your own question, though the only expected answer is 'No', especially when the words are superimposed on a sky-high pile of red rockets beside a collapsed heap of NATO missiles. Against this backdrop, post-Falklands rhetoric may proceed (as in Mills's constituency speeches) to declare that just as 'our' leader was firm in the face of the Argentinians, even so would she not shrink 'to press the button'. This is then backed up by quoting the leader's very own words: 'Labour would not have fired a shot.'

At the risk of seeming to pick linguistic·nits, it's worth looking at how such utterances work. The sentence is half of a 'counterfactual' sentence, with something like 'if Labour had been in government' missing. In some languages such grammatical constructions do not exist:[1] speakers of such languages, confronted with this kind of example in English, are inclined to say 'But it wasn't, so what's the point?' Whether Labour would actually have fired the famous shot is indeed beside the point, as far as a claim to truth is concerned. The real point is rhetorical, and left for the hearer to infer. Presumably the intended point is that the hearer assumes (momentarily at least) that firing the shot (like being *militarist*) is a good thing. Thus is consensus constructed.

Syntactic Tactics
From the beginning of the Falklands crisis, the abstract noun was an important device in the verbal arsenal deployed by politicians and the media – as it always is in any discourse designed to create our categories of reality for us. Their use is highly sophisticated, not to say sophistical, but they possess linguistic properties of great tactical potential. The grand abstractions *Sovereignty* and *Paramountcy* are cut loose from concrete propositions that might be analysed as true or false. To say that someone or something is *sovereign* or *paramount* (in relation to something else) may make some sort of verifiable sense; the two words would also be virtually synonymous. Transform them into nouns and you appear to be staking out separate bits of semantic ground with corresponding bits of reality. Creating the word seems to create the thing:

once created, they can be manoeuvred to form pseudo-explanations of events and states of affairs.[2]

In the course of successive news bulletins concerning the failure of the Peruvian peace initiative, references were made to the Argentinians being 'intransigent'.[3] This was soon nominalised into 'Intransigence', thus attaining a certain status as a causal explanation: the Peruvian plan would have been accepted, it was said, but for Argentine *Intransigence*. The word has an almost identical semantic twin: *Resolution*. The difference is that *Resolution* is British, and is given as the cause of 'our' success. Interestingly, both are alive and well and playing a part in our industrial disputes, or what (in the Falklands afterglow) Mrs Thatcher called our 'economic battles at home' against 'the enemy within'. For trades unions, like 'Argies', commonly demonstrate 'Intransigence', while it is the 'Resolution' of management and government which will 'defeat' them.

After the Falklands crisis the rhetoric and the named abstractions remain. Because their grammatical make-up does not tie them to people, places or things, they can do duty in any context, but especially where war is concerned. Here is part of William Whitelaw's 1982 speech to the annual conference of Civil Defence and Emergency Planning Officers:

> The world has seen our *resolution* in the face of unprovoked *aggression* in the South Atlantic; so too, it has seen our *resolution* to work for a peaceful world; but when all is said and done, we cannot be immune from the risk of war *coming on us* by *misadventure* or *miscalculation*.

Again it is worth looking at what syntactic tactics can do for the speaker of English. What they can do here most potently is to make it possible to avoid any direct reference at all to people as actors causing actions for which they are responsible. In fact, they make it possible to avoid referring to specific people at all. In the world projected by Whitelaw, our friend *Resolution* reappears as a free-floating entity face to face, not, this time, with *Intransigence* but with *Unprovoked Aggression*. (Aggression was often also *naked* in Falklands talk, perhaps because it is more civilised when clothed.) A coherent statement like 'We were resolved to do such and such' has been turned into a thing, *Resolution*, which can be possessed ('our') and even 'seen'. The verbal noun *Aggression* evades reference to the person you think is aggressive in a specific context. It appears as a thing that can be 'in' a place. If it can pop up in the South Atlantic, Whitelaw's syntax implies, it might manifest itself elsewhere too, in the form of the Soviet menace, perhaps.

This is not all. Nouns can collect under their wings a jumble of parts and stick them together by nothing more than semantic glue. Falklands talk used 'the nation', 'the country', in this way. Here we have 'the world'. The coda of Whitelaw's balanced period (its very symmetry lulls one into acceptance) is the most blatant of all his exploitations of the verbal noun. 'Somebody miscalculated' becomes *Miscalculation*. Some of the more 'treacherous' among us (for that is how dissenters were styled by the government at the time) thought that the government had miscalculated in the Falklands war, and may even be said thereby to have been responsible for it. But free-floating *Miscalculation* invites you to place the blame anywhere and everywhere but here, and extends the context of application from the 'South Atlantic' to the European nuclear theatre. Closely related to all this is the trick of making a noun like *war* an actor in its own right instead of the product of human causes. War can just 'come upon us'.

War, Meaning Business

Economic sanctions against Argentina might, it has been plausibly argued, have cut short the occupation of the Falkland Islands in a matter of weeks: 'The simplest weapon – money – was never used against the bankrupt Argentinian junta.'[4] The money-missile was not used because it would have boomeranged upon the financial bastions of the city. Note well the easy metaphorical transfer between the conceptual domains of finance and conflict. If money can be a weapon, war can also be treated as business, and perhaps with greater 'naturalness' in the semantic-conceptual practices our capitalist-militarist culture has created.

The militarisation of rhetoric is part of the general militarisation of our economic and social life in the age of the military-industrial complex. It was common during the Falklands expedition to talk about war in terms of the world of work, to judge fighting by the standards applied in civilian life to work. And it was, and is, common post-Falklands talk to apply to work, strikes and unemployment a military vocabulary. That is the essence of the metaphor – perceiving one area of experience in terms of another.[5] One might be tempted to dismiss it as no more than that, were it not that such metaphors, when they occur systematically, provide a rare window onto the mental worlds of those who use them. Like the categories created by abstract nouns, they are a way of making one kind of sense of reality, and even of getting others to focus on it and act on it in a similar way.

Many different metaphors, comparisons and analogies were used by the media to construct a way of looking at the Falklands war, but none tripped so naturally off the tongue as the metaphor *war is work*. 'In the first exchanges, an Argentine submarine appears to have been hit. All this means that the British forces are *getting on with it...the job* they were sent down to the South Atlantic to do, namely to remove the Argentines...'.[6] The convenient grammar of the passive enables the *Mail* to avoid saying directly who was doing the hitting or the sending down to the South Atlantic. But the editorialist is explicit enough about the forces being employed in a removal job. And a few sentences later, the 'takeover' of South Georgia is said to show the Argentines that 'we mean business'. Even cliches like these constitute a kind of verbal filter, categorising war as an economic venture.

The Falklands 'enterprise', as some papers called it, provided *jobs*, thus turning inside-out the phrase 'the army of the unemployed' (it sounds somewhat odd to say 'the army of the employed'). The word *job*, like its opposite number *unemployment*, is relatively new in its modern sense of steady (rather than piece) work; both words, thrown up in the nineteenth century, reify social problems and generate stereotyped values.[7] The *job* brings all occupations down to a single level, without distinction of worth in product or service, without distinction between creating or killing. Having a job, any job, is good, and the people who 'have' them are good people. And the contrary for *unemployment*, and the people 'in' it. (Interestingly, jobs appear as metaphorically possessed, but unemployment is something you find yourself 'in', metaphorically contained by). The *war is work* metaphor works far more effectively for a 'professional' army than it could for a conscript force. It enters profoundly into human relations. When one of the many and much-quoted army and navy wives was reported as saying 'Yes, I am afraid, but it's his *job*',[8] the metaphor was directly controlling the woman's conception of reality and inducing acceptance of it.

Metaphors tend to spawn themselves in associated clusters. The war-as-business metaphor is revealingly double-edged. Soldiers can be metaphorically spoken of not only as *labour* (and, of course, as the officer-managers beloved of British industry, according to the recruitment propaganda) but also as a *substance*, as a *resource*. Troops are 'poured in' and 'pulled out' like a substance; victories ('successes') achieved by 'working together' have a 'price' and '*cost*' lives'. Another way by which the people who do the fighting are dehumanised is via the conventional attributes of professionalism: 'the bravery and *expertise*…they did their *jobs* calmly and *efficiently*' (*Daily Mail*). But machines also 'work': the papers spoke of the efficiency of the 'war machine'. The troops *gearing* themselves for battle'[9] are not just being though of as getting their 'gear' together, but as machines, as other metaphors in the same paper indicated: 'The British war *machine* [i.e. the troops] went into *overdrive* yesterday.' The strategic advantage of representing individual men as machines or parts of machines is clear.

The work ethos of the Falklands war propaganda was best represented in the most commonplace metaphor of the lot, so commonplace that its content seemed totally neutral and natural: *the Task Force*. This crucial metaphor is reversible: it presents war in terms of economic life, and can be turned round to present economic life in terms of war. This is exactly how industrial rhetoric was militarised in the post-Falklands era. Here is Peregrine Worsthorne doing just that: 'I raised the question as to whether public opinion, excited by the examples of what *task forces* can do 8,000 miles away, would start calling for comparable *assaults* on evils near home like mass unemployment.'[10]

He reorientates the metaphor simply by taking away the capital letters. The original metaphor behind the proper name Task Force is thus revealed, but the military association remains. This is no mere decorative metaphor: it expresses, perhaps even guides, and certainly helps to sell, a prescription for actual policy: 'It would not be surprising...if Mrs Thatcher invited the returning soldiers to have a go at running the railways... – a mere holiday *task* by comparison with what they have been doing recently.' Three weeks later the same paper was making a patriotic appeal for the same solution: 'The Government should allow the nonsense to continue no longer. It should get the Army to provide a minimum...service...; *the country* looks to the Government to *keep life going*, and it will look to the Government to put troops in the driving seats of trains if railmen refuse'.[11]

Economic Battles

Amongst other things, the militarist ethos presumably involves the exaltation of the military values of disciplined obedience to authority, patriotic fervour and ruthless efficiency. This is clearly what some minds see as required in industrial relations. Much of the rhetoric produced by politicians and the media during the Aslef strike depended upon military metaphors and comparisons. Explicit references were made to the professionalism, patriotism and proficiency of the forces. The strike itself was spoken of in the metaphorical cliches of war-fighting – not an unusual thing to do in such situations, of course, but more potent in the post-Falklands context. The *argy-bargy* of the unions had taken on a new meaning. Moreover, once the metaphorical ground is staked out, metaphorical inferences can be left to insinuate themselves into the mind. Aslef strikers (refusing to work) were contrasted with the task force (who had volunteered for their 'work'). Were they, then, the enemy? Was Ray Buckton really Galtieri? Was the 'beleaguered' British Rail Board the innocent victim of aggression? 'Call off the rail strike or we'll call an air strike!' warned a much photographed banner, as the troops returned to the Task Force troopships. The *Sun*'s editorial comment of 30 June declared that a strike by Aslef might smash the rail industry but will 'never break us'. The reason? 'As the battle of the Falklands demonstrated so clearly, *nobody* can break this nation'.[12]

Mrs Thatcher's 'mood of the nation' speech at Cheltenham on 4 July merely had to capitalise on the metaphorical discourse of the moment. The allusive use of a Churchillian rhetoric was itself metaphorical – the audience was being encouraged to see the post-Falklands situation in 1982 in terms of the situation post-World War II. It was a metaphorical organisation of historical reality, and, like all such tricks, it simplified its material by focussing on certain aspects and leaving out the bits which don't fit the desired model. Here it was patriotic unity in work that was focussed on: 'We must find the means and the method of working together not only in times of war and mortal anguish but in times of peace...' To this was added some historical fiction, though the grammar is manipulated to avoid direct statement of fact: 'Why do *we have to be invaded* before we throw aside our selfish aims and begin to *work together?*' The *Guardian* observed (5 July 1982) that the evident message was that 'the nation' had no time for *fainthearts* (a Falklands talk term for those who questioned the sense of sending the Task Force) or troublemakers in industry. 'The nation' was no longer 'in retreat', and by implication was prepared to fight the industrial enemies – the unions – in its midst. There was no explicit identification of the unions with the enemy: the 'economic battles' involve a more abstract enemy. So there was an appeal to the workers, in the spirit of wartime patriotism 'to put his family, his comrades and his country first'. Not only family but also comradeship was thus defined as in opposition to the union. And an appeal to the officer class as well: 'Now was the time for management to *lift its sights* and *lead* with professionalism and effectiveness.'[13]

The military metaphors were not confined to this occasion, but systematically underpinned all press reporting and comment on the Aslef dispute. British Rail had a '*strategy* to *defeat* the train drivers' strike', which involved a worst [case] scenario'. it was all 'A question of *Tactics*' as '*tactical manoeuvring* on both sides enters a complex stage'. British Rail feared lest it appear (like Galtieri?) 'the more *intransigent* party'. Possible '*diversionary effects*' were taken into account. Dismissal was 'a *weapon* to be used with caution'.[14] The *Sunday Telegraph* thought that 'However inept its *tactics* British Rail's management *strategy* had been correct', that 'this unnecessary contest (the Falklands conflict had of course, been 'necessary') cannot be allowed to end in *surrender*', and that 'Sir Peter Parker and his Railways Board had no alternative but to *stand and fight* at last.'[15] As for the unions themselves, having objected to Scargill's reference to 'his lads' as 'contemptuous' (though it had not, apparently, been contemptuous to refer to 'our lads' in the Task Force), the *Telegraph* metaphorically classified them as if they were terrorists, calling them 'industrial *saboteurs*' engaged in '*guerrilla* tactics' and causing 'mayhem'.

Once the railways had 'dug in' for what was frequently referred to as a 'siege', cries of anguish at the consequences of economic battle were raised. In the House (14 July 1982) Denis Howell declared that 'those who have given *comfort and succour to this strike* [in the usual cliché it is "to the enemy" carry an immense responsibility for all this *damage* and all this *suffering*'. He called for 'a halt to the *destruction*', and spoke of the duty of all those who believe the public should be *protected*', and of impending '*disaster*'. The *Times*, too, talked of union members 'holding firm in their ranks', being *'strategically* placed', causing *'dangers'* and being 'ready and able to *inflict damage'*.[16]

George Gardiner, Conservative member for Reigate, had been most concerned about the *'civilians'* in this 'economic battle'. 'If ever a campaign medal was deserved by civilians in time of peace, it must be the...daily rail commuters who in the vicious weather of last winter did everything in their power to get to work regardless, rather then resigning themselves to *defeat...'*

Eventually, *'peace terms'* were arrived at. As far as the unions were concerned, it was a 'return-to-work formula which amounted to *surrender'*. The union had 'faced *implacable resistance* from the British Rail Board, backed by the Government'. British Rail's *'battle* to regain the confidence of its customers' had been won, despite the *'pockets of resistance* to flexible rostering' that remained. (*Daily Telegraph*, 19 July 1982). Aslef and the TUC were left muttering their own class-war rhetoric: Buckton's *'battle'* had been lost through *'betrayals'*; Aslef's decision was not a *'defeat'* for the union...Meanwhile the imperialist war rhetoric drowned their voices. 'The Defeat of Aslef' was announced by the *Daily Telegraph*. It would be more difficult now for the TUC 'to mount an effective *attack'* on Tebbit's bill. The prospect of unemployment would 'force unions onto the *defensive'*. After Port Stanley, the papers had called for the government to 'build on its success'; echoing this phrase, the *Telegraph* invited the government to 'build on its victory'.[17]

The metaphor that lies behind these quotes, and many other similar ones, is that *industrial disputes are war*. The logic of the metaphor was used in this instance by the media to imply that patriotic civilians would be on the side of government and management. It is a common enough ploy. We have had wars on poverty, wars on crime, battles with inflation, and so on. Faced with the energy crisis, President Carter declared it was 'the moral equivalent of war.' Such metaphors highlight certain aspects of reality. But they are not merely ways of viewing reality. Certain views of reality can lead to, or at least justify, ways of acting. Carter's metaphor was certainly bound up with policy.[18]

A crucial element in the 'war on X' formula is the setting up of an alien, an enemy, that will unite all right-thinking people. That in itself involves a metaphorical process: complicated sets of historical facts and forces get reduced to simple, personified entities. These ingredients – the militarisation of rhetoric and the grand abstraction – tend to crop up at the economic trouble spots. When they do, they often reveal the extent to which metaphor and policy are bound up with one another. 'The Front Line Against Youth Unemployment' (*Telegraph*,[19] July 1982) might look like merely a decorative phrase at first glance. The contents of the ensuing article, however, show that the military metaphor and the abstract noun ('youth unemployment') are important elements of an ideology. The latter is an indispensible term for a most serious phenomenon, namely unemployed youths). But, combined with the war metaphor, the term reflects politically specific views of what 'youth unemployment' is and how it can be 'combatted'.

All this is likely to be dismissed as 'mere semantics' – the conventional defence of those who dislike having what they say treated as what they mean. Is it all no more than a way of talking? No less an apologist of the Right than Peregrine Worsthorne has made this point: 'One should never underestimate the power of the talking classes to impose their idea of reality' (*Sunday Telegraph*, 20 June 1982). There is one crucial distinction, of course. Worsthorne believes that the only classes who 'talk' are composed of soft leftish liberals who distort reality, whereas he and his friends know what the one and true reality really is. In fact all *classes* talk; only some have more power than others to get their talk through the media. That means getting their reality through the media; at least in part, that means getting their metaphors into circulation.

8

Nukespeak:
Aspects of the
Language of the Cold War

1. In the Beginning

In the beginning was the Bomb. *The Times* of 7 August 1945 carried the following report:

> Mr Truman personally made the announcement about the bomb to officers of the Augusta in the wardroom. He said 'the *experiment* has been an overwhelming *success*'.

Three days later, *The Times* reported the American general, General Spaatz, as announcing:

> The second *use* of the atomic bomb *occurred* at noon August 9th at Nagasaki. Crew members report *good results*. No further details will be available until the mission returns.[1]

I take these to be probably the first public examples of Nukespeak. As the full enormity of Hiroshima and Nagasaki dawned upon the world, and even dawned upon the editors of *The Times*, the full resources of linguistic deception and self-deception were marshalled; they have been thus marshalled ever since. It was impossible to conceal the facts totally, but it *was* possible to disguise them in specious language. Forty odd years of this kind of verbal screening seem to have habituated many people to the menace of atomic and nuclear weapons. As Edward Thompson has pointed out,

> the deformation of culture begins with language itself...A certain kind of 'realist' and 'technical' vocabulary effects a closure which seals out the imagination, and prevents the reason from following the most manifest sequence of cause and consequence.[2]

This seems to pinpoint the essence of what we are calling Nukespeak. But to get an idea of how such a sublanguage comes into being and works in practice, we can best go back to George Orwell, who gave us the word and the concept of Newspeak. In his novel *Nineteen Eighty-Four* Orwell describes a centralised repressive and militarised state in which the rulers attempt to control thought itself by controlling language, by creating new words and grammatical rules:

> The purpose of Newspeak was not only to provide a medium of expression to the world-view and mental habits proper to the devotees [of the dominant ideology], but to make all other modes of thought impossible.[3]

The theory behind this is that the vocabulary and grammar of the language you speak actually determine and delimit the thoughts you can think and influence the actions you perform. This is a view of language known to linguistics as the Whorfian hypothesis (after the linguist B.L. Whorf), and in its extreme form very few linguists would want to endorse it.[4] It leaves out too much of the creative freedom in human language. And it can lead to absurd and damaging claims – for instance, the claim that because a certain language has no separate words for 'blue' or 'green' the speakers of that language cannot see blue and green as different colours. However, Orwell's basic idea – that language can influence thinking – *does* make a great deal of sense if you bear in mind a few points about the nature of language and language use in particular societies. To start with, a language like English is not an entirely neutral system. Whole chunks of vocabulary and grammatical habits are produced by groups with special interests (politicians, bureaucrats, advertisers, and so on). The consumers of language then consume it, by and large unconsciously and uncritically.

The question is: does this fact influence what people can think and do? The answer is: not necessarily, because it *is possible* to think your way round received words. But my guess is that *most* people don't or won't think round and beyond the language they consume, or maybe have not acquired the skill to do so. So they use whatever words and phrases they are given and endlessly exchange the concepts attached to them. What I am suggesting is that the words and grammar of a language can codify a view of the world (including a view of nuclear arms), and that when people use 'their' language, the language itself confirms, reinforces or even directs people's attitudes and beliefs.

If that is so, then we are not all that far from Orwell's world of *Nineteen Eighty-Four*, and language does indeed play a subtle role in the direction of thought, alongside the other devices of western propaganda systems. The purpose of these propaganda systems is, to quote Noam Chomsky, 'to fix the limits of possible thought'.[5] True, there is no state propaganda department rewriting the dictionaries and proscribing undesirable words in the hope of dictating what people can think. Nevertheless, a specific ideological sublanguage like Nukespeak does emerge within particular national institutions and is disseminated by them. Let's take some concrete examples of the various subtle and not-so-subtle ways in which words and phrases are manipulated.

The most obvious area to look at is the armed forces and the bureaucracies that serve them. It is here that the men who plan and perform the killing apparently have a need to be linguistically anaesthetised. A well-known example from this area is the term 'pacification'. To quote Orwell again:

> Defenceless villages are bombarded from the air, the inhabitants driven out ... into countryside, the cattle machine-gunned, the huts set on fire with incendiary bullets ... this is called pacification.[6]

The Americans were particular adept at 'pacification' during the Vietnam war, and at many other related activities such as 'protective reactions' (bombing raids) and 'urbanization' (the destruction of peasant villages).

In Nukespeak there are many similar terms: weapons of mass destruction are referred to as 'hardware' or 'devices' or, worse, 'deterrents'. The vague term 'strike' is now regularly used to mean a specifically nuclear attack. Military jargon of this type amounts to a semi-secret language: it has a precise meaning for the initiated but constitutes a misleading smoke-screen for the general public. In addition, such terms are basically euphemisms: one may or may not know precisely what they refer to, but either way one is desensitised to the reality of means of distracting associations.

The grotesque nicknames given to nuclear bombs and their so-called 'delivery' systems go even further. It was a bomb called 'Little Boy' which destroyed Hiroshima. It was 'Fat Man' who (or rather which) devastated Nagasaki. We are presumably supposed to regard them as innocent, even endearing. And then there is a missile that can carry up to ten times the explosive power of the 'Little Boy' and is known as a 'tomahawk'. The effect, again, is to minimise the horrific destructiveness of the thing – Indian tomahawks are, after all, scarcely more than playthings. NATO soldiers are also armed with 'lances' – equally primitive-sounding weapons, although in reality they are artillery missiles that can carry nuclear or neutron bombs.

A classical education is useful in the Nukespeak business. *Titan*, *Poseidon* and *Trident* are names which, unlike 'tomahawk' and 'lance', permit you to acknowledge the gigantic inhumanity of the things they refer to – but at the same time confer on them a kind of cultural respectability, and even hint at supernatural powers. And to what extent, one wonders, is a certain kind of English mind influenced by an unconscious feeling that Britannia is incomplete without her Trident? But the coining of words can do more even than this. It can create a whole universe of dubious entities and categories.

This is particularly the case with pseudo-technical classifications, which impose a purely linguistic grid on the real world.

Take the threefold classification of nuclear weapons into strategic, tactical and theatre weapons. This is an entirely verbal con-trick. Anyone with the slightest information on weapons systems can see that there are no clear-cut dividing lines between these categories. But the purpose of the con-trick is clear. It is to insinuate into our minds the notion that there are different kinds of nuclear war-fighting, and that allegedly 'limited' nuclear war is possible because it is sayable. The term 'limited' itself is, of course, one of the most dangerous devices in the Nukespeak arsenal.

The danger is that such terms enter everyday discourse and direct people's utterances and thus their thoughts. Undoubtedly the most pervasive Nukespeak term, and the most potent, is the term *deterrent*. There's a lot to say about the semantics of 'deterrence'. But the main thing to say about it is that, in spite of its simple appearance, the word presents an extremely dense conceptual package of the kind Marcuse called 'telescoped' or 'abridged thought'.[7]

Roughly, you can undo the package like this: for people who link up the noun *deterrent* with the verb *deter* (and there may be people who don't), a common phrase like 'the British deterrent' seems to imply: 'There exists a British nuclear something-or-other which causes the Russians not to do something awful to us.' That's not all, because it seems to commit you also to assuming that the Russians are *in fact* about to do something awful, and would do it, if the 'deterrent' weren't there.

I have stated the case somewhat crudely, but the point is that the single word *deterrent* wraps up a whole cold-war ideology and presents as implicitly true a proposition which is highly contentious, to say the least. The very word 'effects a closure' on debate.

The other major breeding-ground for Nukespeak is the established media. One of the media's propaganda functions is to disseminate the kind of terminology we've just been discussing and ensure that it gets into general circulation. But another important function is to deal with awkward facts and events which conflict with what the dominant view of the social reality is or ought to be. These awkward events may be riots on the British streets; they may be the inhumane slaughter of civilians by an ally. Such things are not supposed to happen, and newspapers do their best to explain them away, or rather to talk them away, by pulling the linguistic wool over their readers' eyes. I'd like to return to *The Times* of August 1945 to give some idea of how vocabulary, grammar and rhetoric have combined to distort and reinterpret the atomic bombing of Japan, in an evident attempt to relieve the conscience. What *The Times*'s editors did was to give visual and verbal prominence to the scientific and technological 'achievement' of the bomb. And they did so in terms which made it appear that a divine revelation of the nature of the universe had been vouchsafed to God's chosen people. More than that, during the course of a series of extraordinary leading articles, the atom bomb, patently an instrument of indiscriminate massacre, was verbally transmuted into a 'power' capable bringing not death but *life*. Furthermore, not only the *invention* of the thing, but also its *use*, was made to look like an inevitable natural process in which human beings had scarcely any responsibility. True, the paper calls for what it termed 'responsible control of this terrible power', but only after it had interpreted the bomb for its readers as an essentially beneficient gift to mankind:

> The fundamental power of the universe, the power manifested in the sunshine ... the sustaining force of earthly life, is entrusted [by whom, one might ask] at last to human hands.[8]

As for the details of the actual destruction, such accounts as penetrated the dust cloud were reported to be no more than Japanese propaganda and dismissed with the contemptuous understatement English is so good at.

One of the oldest tricks of political rhetoric is to present the victims of an action as if they themselves had caused it. According to *The Times*, if the 'Japanese' were bombed, then they had only themselves to blame. Such an assertion was possible because the distinction between Japanese rulers and Japanese civilians was systematically blurred by the way language was used.

> Japanese leaders have no alternative open to them but the direct approach of unconditional surrender. The longer they postpone it the more terrible the destruction that will fall upon the heads of the Japanese nation.[9]

The reality behind the words is the threat to incinerate thousands of civilians. But notice how the grammar conceals this: the use of the noun 'destruction' makes it possible to avoid saying who *does* the destruction. In fact, no one at all appears to cause it – destruction just '*falls*', as if it were some natural cataclysm attributable to divine retribution. It's not just the words, it's the grammatical phrasing that distorts and disguises reality for a hurried or uncritical reader. A typical trick in Newspeak, Orwell tells us, is to avoid verbs or turn them into nouns. Why should this be so? Because if you avoid verbs you can avoid saying who is doing the action to *whom*, and *when*. If you *do* have to use a verb, you can always choose one that doesn't require an explicit human subject or agent.

Headline writers are well practised in these techniques. I shall conclude with a rapid look at *The Times* headlines for 7 and 10 August 1945. The headline for the 7th runs:

> FIRST ATOMIC BOMB HITS JAPAN...
> ...'RAIN OF RUIN' FROM THE AIR[10]

The verb 'hits' has 'atomic bomb' as its grammatical subject; there is no sign of the human agents who caused the event, nor any sign that the event was intentional; it might even appear to be accidental. The grammatical object (or victim) of the verb is not the inhabitants of Hiroshima, but the vague 'Japan' – a term that implied treachery and evil for *The Times* at that period. The cruel phrase used by Truman ('rain of ruin') confirms the impression that the event was somehow natural - or even supernatural, because there's a kind of biblical overtone to the phrase. Atom bombs, like floods and thunderstorms, begin to look like acts of God.

On 10 August, the Nagasaki bomb, apparently less newsworthy, was reported in a relatively inconspicuous position on the page with the following headlines:

ATOM BOMB ON NAGASAKI
SECOND CITY HIT

As before, no human agent is referred to; there's not even a verb in the first line, and the relationship between the bomb and Nagasaki is compressed into the inexplicit word *on*. We're not even told it's a second *bomb* – that could be embarrassing – nor what the city was hit *by*. All this obfuscation is made possible by manipulating the everyday passive construction – a grammatical construction of great utility to the propagandist, since it allows you to suppress the agents and instruments of actions. You may say that the details I claim are suppressed or distorted are obvious in the context, and that journalists only write like this for reasons of economy. But I would want to suggest that such minutiae of phrasing are significant because they both reflect the mental posture of the writer *and* conceivably influence, or at least confirm, the mental posture of the reader. This is precisely the kind of thing which seems to me to be fundamental to the way thought is moulded in the propaganda processes that exist in our society.[11]

2. The Rhetoric of the New Cold War

Since 1945, many of the original features of Nukespeak have remained in use and evolved; new areas of grammar and vocabulary have also been exploited. Yet the most obvious difference between 1945 and 1984 is the communications explosion. The proliferation of electronic media has made the manipulation of language even more crucial, both in the international and domestic context. A variety of linguistic practices can be seen operating for two audiences and two ends. On the one hand, they contribute towards domestic perceptions of the Soviet threat: on the other, they count as concrete actions in international diplomacy by defining and creating a particular verbal relationship between East and West. This is probably the most important aspect in the analysis of Nukespeak, although both were much in evidence during Margaret Thatcher's visit to North America in the week ending 1 October 1983. There are extraordinarily complex factors governing the perception and interpretation of public utterance both at home and abroad, but analysis of the construction of the utterances themselves is none the less important in establishing their potential range of significance; such analysis can indeed end up as a political act in its own right. The context of that week of megaphone rhetoric is crucial. Cruise and Pershing II missiles were to be deployed in West Europe at the end of the year. Some weeks previously, the Russians had shot down a Korean airliner and claimed that it had been spying. The European peace movements were planning demonstrations in the coming months. Reagan had recently made certain conditional offers on weapon deployment; Andropov had stridently rejected them as spurious.

The first thing that a political leader will do when facing actual or potential opposition is to assert a superior claim to virtue. Hence Margaret Thatcher stated in Washington: 'We must not fall into the trap of projecting our own morality on to the Soviet leaders.' Such statements are difficult to counter because their force lies in covert implications that depend on the hearers' knowledge and beliefs. Perhaps the best way to deal with them is precisely by analysing the rhetorical tricks they deploy. So who are *we*, who *must not fall into the trap?* If she says 'must not', that must mean there is an actual danger of our doing so. Or, if this is not an all-inclusive 'we', then she must mean that there is a danger of some people falling into the trap. Who are they? Presumably the peace movements, or those who are gullible and/or weak enough to fall into 'traps'. This ambiguity is matched by the ambiguity of the phrase 'the trap' itself. It's open to you to assume that the trap must have been set by someone. By whom? Either the Soviets or the peace movements – or, to take another step in the chain of implications, both conspiring together. There is ambivalence, too, in the way *morality* and *ethics* are used in the speech. At one point it is implied that Soviet morality is merely different from 'ours', at another that Soviet morality is absent altogether. This deliberately blurs rational distinctions and discourages exploration of relative viewpoints. No nonsense about the other side's point of view, relative standards, subjective perceptions!

The claim to moral superiority is further hammered home by two rhetorical tools: the repetition of quasi-factual assertions, each one being a near paraphrase of the preceding one, and all offered from the standpoint of supposedly superior knowledge as well as superior virtue; and the use of a series of rhetorical questions, with both implicit and explicit answers. It was offered as a fact that

> They do not share our aspirations.
> They are not constrained by our ethics.
> They have always considered themselves exempt from the rules that bind other nations.
> They pose as champions of free nations ...

These are all grammatically or semantically negative and imply the assumption that 'we' do have valid aspirations and ethics, that we do abide by the rules, etc. The rhetorical questions are really repetitions of the same basic propositions, with the difference that the negative statements are (to begin with) not spoken. The speaker expects the hearer to know the answer and to accept it as going without being said.

Is there conscience in the Kremlin? [No, of course there isn't!]
Do they ever ask themselves what is the purpose of life? [Of course they never ask themselves, but *we* do, and we know the right answer, too.]
Does the way they handled the Korean airliner atrocity suggest that they ever considered such questions? [Just in case anyone has got it wrong, here comes the answer]
No
Their clique is barren of conscience!

The unspoken assumptions are glossed in the brackets. Which is where we came in. A fairly moderate degree of linguistic awareness reveals the ritual, almost liturgical, quality of such verbiage. No serious assessment of the urgent problem of the Soviet Union can be done on such a basis.

In addition to portraying the Russians as 'ruthless automatons' (to quote the *Daily Mail*'s gloss) for the benefit of domestic audiences, the speech also contributed to the East–West dialogue by defining that dialogue as dialogue of a specific kind. It did so by utilising a dominant metaphor of our culture:[12] namely, *argument is war*. The state of the dialogue was redefined in archaic military terms as a *duel* between national champions, and in archaic mythic terms as a *struggle* between the forces of good and evil. The starting point was Andropov's speech of the previous week, part of which Thatcher quoted (out of context and without authority for the translation):

A struggle is under way for the hearts and minds of billions of people on the planet, and the future of mankind depends ... on the outcome of the ideological struggle.

Grammatically, this is a declarative assertion of alleged fact. Pragmatically, we want to know what sort of communication it is, what sort of speech act is being performed. Thatcher told us: 'That is Mr Andropov's *challenge*. I accept it.' In societies where the duel is or was an institution, the challenge and the acceptance were highly ritualised pieces of verbal (and non-verbal) behaviour. That, no doubt, is calculated to be its appeal on the home front. Now clearly, in a sense, Andropov asked for it. Socialised humans answer questions compulsively, respond to calls, orders, and all manner of verbal stimuli. But the point is that, in international communication, it is not *necessary* to behave in irrational ways. After all, bluffs can be called, questions questioned, statements doubted. Moreover, the specific force of an utterance is not usually unambiguously determined by its grammatical form. In the case of the Andropov quote, you *can* respond to it as a pious platitude. To respond to it as a *challenge* is to make a strictly unnecessary choice to increase tension rather than to reduce it. Contradictory and self-contradictory utterances and speech acts are of great interest, as the media watchfulness for such things testifies. Sometimes, however, they are not easy to disentangle without a little (really very little) linguistic reflection. One obvious case in that week of megaphone diplomacy was the voice of Vice-President Bush, suggesting that Britain and France might at some time include their nuclear weapons in arms control talks. What was the intention and intended effect of this? It was very easy for spokesmen to put the confusion down precisely to 'misinterpretation' of the intended speech effect.[13] Meanwhile Mrs Thatcher's interpretation of Mr Andropov held good. A British minister (apparently less concerned about saving Mr Bush's face) claimed that the Vice-President was simply wrong by invoking what is now a classic Nukespeak confidence trick: the purely verbal distinction between *strategic* and *tactical* weapons. Before French and British weapons could be included in talks on *intermediate nuclear forces*, they would have to be rechristened 'tactical'.

Contradictions inside Mrs Thatcher's own speeches of the week in question are more significant: they point to basic flaws (perhaps intentional) in the rhetoric of the *zero option/dual track* policy. While on the one hand adopting a defiant and threatening posture towards the Soviet leadership, on the other hand Mrs Thatcher insisted that negotiations should be pursued. We have here two contradictory speech acts, two contradictory psychological messages. This is typical of the nuclear diplomacy of the last few years, up to and including the various 'offers' made by Reagan (and Andropov) during the 1983 Geneva INF negotiations. However genuine they might be, the dual proposal not to deploy Cruise and Pershing II missiles if and only if SS20s (and SS4s and SS5s) are withdrawn – and, conversely, the proposal to withdraw SS20s (and SS4s and SS5s) if and only if Cruise and Pershing II missiles are not deployed – are linguistically, psychologically and diplomatically counter-productive. The reason is that they consist in combinations of incompatible speech acts: promises and threats. In some crucial respects, promises and threats are paradoxically similar. They both commit you (unless they are 'idle' or 'insincere') to a certain course of action by the mere utterance of a conventionally agreed formula of words. In one equally crucial respect they are, however, diametrically opposed: promises undertake to do something believed to be in the hearer's interests, while threats undertake to do something believed *not* to be in their interests. Threats are usually conditional, promises not primarily or necessarily conditional. It is interesting that in English the word 'promise' can be used to utter a threat: 'If you dare say that again, I promise you I'll give you a thrashing!' The basic form of the zero option/dual track 'offer' is this: 'I promise that I will not deploy *x*, if you withdraw *y*.'

Now this is a grammatically negative sentence, and there is a certain body of psychological and psycholinguistic research[14] that seems to show that humans process positive grammatical structures more quickly and easily than their negative counterparts. It is possible that the negative dual-track offer somehow gets reprocessed in the course of communication as a sentence with a positive 'promise': 'I promise that I will deploy x, if you do not withdraw y.' Despite the word 'promise', this is what most people would call a threat. So are zero option/dual track 'offers' conditional promises or conditional threats? This is what is meant by the idea that moves in nuclear diplomacy nearly always contain incompatible speech acts. The American psychologist, Charles Osgood, has pointed this out in connection with his proposal for a policy of Graduated and Reciprocal Initiatives in Tension Reduction or GRIT. One of the rules for GRIT is that 'Unilateral initiatives must be designed and communicated so as to emphasise a sincere intend to reduce tensions.' In other words, 'Escalation and de-escalation strategies must not be "mixed" ... The reason is psychological: reactions to *threats* [e.g. 'We will deploy Cruise ...'] are incompatible with reactions *to promises* [e.g. 'We will not deploy Cruise ...']; *each strategy thus destroys the credibility of the other.*'[15] Consistency is important, and in this sense Reagan and Thatcher are correct to require western unanimity: it is not good being conciliatory at one point and aggressive at another, and it's even worse to be both simultaneously.

The net result of dual-track-type utterances is an increase in tension and stress. As Osgood also points out, tension and stress tend to decrease flexibility, subtlety and creativity in decision-making. One manifestation of this is what some psychologists have termed 'groupthink', where group decision-making under stress is notable for 'a deterioration of mental efficiency, reality testing, and moral judgement that results from in-group pressures'. Loyalty to the group comes to be considered 'the highest form of morality'. Members of the group thinking under stress evade points of view that might imply that 'This fine group of ours, with its humanitarianism and its high-minded principles, might be capable of adopting a course of action that is inhumane and immoral.'[16] Any tension-producing moves, verbal or otherwise, will lead to less flexible thinking. The dual-track rhetoric, I want to argue, was a major tension-producing way of responding to the Soviet acquisition of approximate nuclear parity. As tension is increased by such rhetoric, so thinking decreases in flexibility; as thinking decreases in flexibility, so cold-war stereotypes grow more lurid, and so each side's conviction of its own righteousness grows. As the stereotypes and self-righteousness grows, so do adversarial postures and tension. The circle is vicious.

A particular kind of tension was generated within the various groupings that loosely constitute the Western peace movement opposed to nuclear weapons deployment in general. In analysing the zero option utterance we have so far assumed that the context of that particular discourse consisted in *two* participants: the Soviet Union, and the United States or their representatives and agents. However, as we have seen, the utterances themselves were auto-destructive – at least in the sense that they seem not to have been designed to receive a positive response. Indeed it has been widely claimed that the negotiating postures referred to by the phrase 'zero option' 'could not provide the basis for serious negotiations and was not meant to do so'.[17]

So what *was* the intention? One inference would be that the intention was to irritate the Russians and further exacerbate existing tension. States might issue such utterance for various purposes, including incitement to war (such speech acts and the circumstance of their issuance would merit investigation). But it is important not to oversimplify the context of discourse, and thus the intentions behind it. In this instance, the Soviet Union was not the sole recipient of the message. There was also 'the general public' and, more specifically, the peace movements themselves. There are thus at least two dialogues going on, interfering with one another and generating paradoxes, dilemmas, contradictions and binds within a system of choices (essentially two-valued) set up by those who set up the discourse itself.[18] For suppose the peace movement refused to accept the utterance as valid (in part because of the linguistic considerations discussed above.) That is, suppose it invoked Habermas's idea of 'validity claims', which we discussed above, and challenged the presumed sincerity of the utterance, as well perhaps as its intelligibility and even the speaker's right to have made it at all. The refusal is *itself* open to the imputation of implicatures: namely, that the peace movement rejected the conditions of the 'offer' (the withdrawal of the Soviet intermediate-range missiles), and thus the further implicature that the peace movement favours the retention of Soviet missiles and is on the Soviet side. I have spoken of implicatures here, but they are not automatic, and seem to require activation and formulation by a sufficiently powerful participant in the discourse (in this case, official government agencies capable of influencing media reporting).

If the peace movement rejected the validity of the zero-option utterance, then, it risked encouraging the interpretation that it was pro-Soviet – and thus contradicting itself, since the vast (unaligned) majority of the movement had in no way condoned Soviet SS20s. The alternative, however, was to accept the validity of the zero-option offer, in which case the interpretation promoted would have made the peace movement out to be in favour of the deployment of Cruise and Pershing II missiles and thus pro-US. In short, the terms of the discourse were: either support the Soviet Union or support the US. A zero-option indeed! In these circumstances (which remain the dominant limits of discourse), it was virtually impossible to express a non-aligned position – not, of course, impossible to find words to say it, but to find the means to be heard saying it. Even if one did get to be heard, it is arguable that the dominant two-valued discourse in which the public is schooled would make the message incomprehensible or unacceptable without the imposition of the binary interpretation. The general point here is that the political bind in which the European peace movements found themselves was generated by the pragmatics of the discourse, skewed as they were in favour of those with power to use public communications media to make the first moves in a sequence of utterances. And it is in such cases that Habermas's notion of the 'ideal speech situation', discussed in Chapter 2, becomes highly relevant.

Let us characterise the speech situation in question more closely, though still informally. It was the United States organs that had, or abrogated, the 'right' in this publicly mediated conversational exchange to formulate the zero-option formula. The peace movements had the 'obligation' to respond. (Silence would also have had meaning.) Such is the nature of the verbal exchange. That obligation was assumed and underscored when prominent spokespersons of the European peace movements were telephoned for their responses minutes after President Reagan had made his zero-option speech. One function of those calls was to ensure that the secondary (perhaps it was politically primary) dialogue between government and protest movement was set in train alongside the overtly intended interaction with the Soviet diplomatic receiver. In this secondary (or primary) dialogue, if someone utters a verbal demand, the pressure of human discourse requires a response; one cannot comfortably stay quiet; so considerable advantage in power goes to whoever is the demander. The peace movements, with their slender resources, were also unable to mount instant conferences, cabinets or committees to establish consensus amongst themselves. Nor, in any case, could they claim the media space (that is, in pragmatic terms, claim a turn in the ongoing mediated conversation of the nations) to state the qualified and nuanced response that *was* formulated. There was, in the democratic pluralist West, freedom to try to be heard (we are grateful for that), but that freedom is limited by the distortions of discourse power. The one thing that the power structure of discourse ruled out altogether, of course, was the valid uttering by the peace movements of a counter-proposal (offer, bid, etc.), which is what the qualified nuanced proposal referred to above would have amounted to. In effect, the type of speech acts permitted the peace movement spokespersons were limited to those of a subordinate respondant role.

The outcome of this exchange was that the unaligned opponents of nuclear deployment were made to appear favourable to the Soviet position, since their response came across as confused, hesitating, but certainly critical of the US. That interpretation of the response was consolidated by both Western and Communist broadcasts in Europe, and the whole forced association of the peace movement with the Soviet Union provided a major part of the pseudo-justification for the Conservative slogan about 'one-sided' disarmament and jibes about Russian stooges that were so effective during the election campaign of 1983.

3. Counter-Nukespeak

There are perhaps lessons in all this for the language used by the peace movement, though much more thought needs to be given to this problem. Because *peace* is a *positively* perceived thing, the government's nuclear propaganda has always been careful to insist that its policies are for *peace*. This has been particularly important for them in a period where there has been increasing public awareness that nuclear strategies have evolved into war-fighting strategies and nuclear technology into war-fighting technology. 'We are the true peace movement' was an effective slogan reiterated by government ministers in the spring of 1983 – effective not only because it asserted an association with peace, but also because it asserted an association with truth. In addition to what was actually said, there was the inference that the 'peace movement' was not 'true', and was thus 'false' or 'dishonest'. Because *war*, on the other hand, may be negatively perceived (this is obviously not always the case, as the Falklands campaign demonstrated), the government, and the media that support it, systematically seek to associate the peace movement with conflict, dissension, aggression and the precipitation of war itself. The *Daily Express*, for example, described a CND demonstration in a banner headline as 'The Peace War'. This is a metaphor: it invites you to see peace (or rather those who wish to be associated with peace) in terms of war, and all that it conjures up. War is such a well-entrenched basis for metaphor in our culture that this can apparently be done to the point of paradox, as in this example, without readers or hearers finding it incongruous. The slogan 'War is Peace' was not found incongruous by the inhabitants of 'Airstrip One' in Orwell's *Nineteen Eighty-Four*. Notice, however, that 'the peace war' is merely some sort of extension of quite habitual phrases like 'election battle' and 'peace campaign', in which aspects of democratic action are treated as aspects of military action.

While the pro-nuclear lobby has been careful to state its case in positively perceived terms (that is, in terms that arouse positive feelings and thus tend to get more readily processed), the peace movement has been obliged for a variety of reasons to state *its* case in predominantly negative terms. In the current climate of discourse, the word 'disarmament' and the older phrase 'ban the bomb' can be linguistic liabilities. Both *disarm* and *ban* are inherently negative, and Osgood's research suggests that it is simply less easy for people to get the meaning of terms which are either grammatically or emotionally negative.[19] Both words imply an act of deprivation; the main problem is that they can be used to imply nothing more than deprivation. This fact has been exploited by government propaganda, which has claimed that nuclear disarmament would leave us without any security arrangements at all. This rests on a tacit implication that 'defence' equals 'nuclear defence'. As for the term 'unilateral disarmament', it was a clever stroke of the public relations people to systematically replace it in official speeches with the phrase 'one-sided disarmament'. 'One-sided' does not have a literal meaning in everyday speech; it is usually used in connection with moral judgements and has distinctly negative connotations. The problem with the term 'unilateralism' is well known. It is taken to be opposite to 'multilateralism', in the sense that *alive* is opposite to *dead*, *open* to *closed*, etc. It is normally contradictory to say e.g. 'the door is open and closed'. Not all pairs of apparent opposites, however, are mutually exclusive: a small elephant is a big animal. And a unilateralist can be a multilateralist and vice versa. There is a natural polarising tendency at work here, which is found throughout language use, but which is especially prominent in cold war polemic. There is another semantic disadvantage in the phrase 'unilateral disarmament' which has been exploited by official criticism. Words with the suffix -*ment* do not unambiguously indicate either a state or an action. The fact that adding -*ment* yields a noun, tends to make actions thing-like and state-like: cf. *payment*, *statement*, etc.

Even when an action is clearly indicated, English does not indicate whether the action is a single act, a series of acts or a continuous process. The word 'disarmament' can thus be understood to refer to a sudden single act of abandonment. There is one final problem with the word, a problem of a symbolic and cultural order: to throw away one's weapons symbolises cowardice and submission.

It is difficult not to become enmeshed in these often irrational webs of meaning when engaging in public discourse. It is as well to be aware of what may be involved. It is less easy to see a solution, but one pragmatic option is to develop discourse around the (predominantly) positively perceived word *defence*. This is already happening at the level of extended argument in the report of the Alternative Defence Commission. Phrases like 'defence without the bomb' and 'nuclear-free defence' carry the positive presupposition that there *is* defence without nuclear weapons. However, because of the principle of least effort, which requires that frequently used meanings need one-word formulations, there is a vocabulary gap waiting to be filled. One recent coinage, 'transarmament' (transition from one stage of decreasing violence to another), unfortunately, is likely to be misunderstood (because of the unusual sense of the prefix *trans*-). Osgood's acronym GRIT has some advantages, thought its expanded form is cumbersome.

Another psychological problem that peace-movement discourse is up against has to do with reinforcement principles. These are well documented by psychologists working on the effectiveness of either positive or negative reinforcement in inducing changes in thinking and behaving.[20] There are two pairs of correlated principles that are relevant. First, immediate reinforcement (sweets now) is more effective than remote reinforcement (toothache tomorrow). Second, concrete reinforcement is more effective than symbolic reinforcement. What relevance might this have for the nuclear debate? The odds are currently in the pro-nuclear government's favour, as far as popular conceptions are concerned, since immediate and concrete rewards can be claimed to accrue from the possession of nuclear weapons: for instance, jobs, trade and political prestige. The odds are largely stacked against peace movements, to the extent that the nuclear facts they have to refer to are remote and symbolic. Missiles are never seen, only spoken about, and then often in symbolic ways (Trident for Britannia; Peacekeeper; Tornado, etc); nuclear proliferation, the possibility of war through accident or design, are potential but not actual threats. This, combined with the psychological principle of denial,[21] whereby the mental apparatus is defended from threatening stimuli by the withdrawal of attention, makes it difficult to communicate about the *dangers* of nuclear arms races.[22]

9

Metaphors and Models of International Relations

It might seem at first sight, and to some people, that a concern with language and linguistic practices is somehow frivolous or 'soft' in the context of the Realpolitik of the nuclear age. However, it is one of the fruits of the research into language use in recent years that the supposed distinction between words and deeds has been dissolved. Speech act theory has given us just that – a theory of speech as act. We can now bridge the gap implied in (Goethe's) Faust's defiant phrase: 'In the beginning was the deed.' The branch of linguistics known as 'pragmatics' has produced detailed accounts of the principles and patterns of language viewed as *behaviour* in concrete contexts of interaction, as the putting into action of one's knowledge of language in situations of different types, for purposes of different types and between actor-speakers of different types and status. This professional research has, however, tended to be mechanistic, and certainly apolitical and dissociated from the ethics of communication-action. One aim of this chapter, therefore, is to urge that a linguistic pragmatics of international communication is needed in order that we can begin to understand and become more responsible for the communicational component in international conflict and cooperation.

Influential personages from the pro-nuclear-deterrence camp from time to time make public claims about language, sometimes to give an air of scientific or scholarly respectability to what are in essence ideological discourses. Perhaps theorists of language are not after all confined to the Academy, to the language laboratories of Swift's Lagado, or, like Syme, to the ranks of Orwell's inner-party language-engineers. Perhaps those with an interest in power and control are naturally led to theorise about language, even to propagate their theories, as part of the ideological edifice upon which their linguistic and non-linguistic actions rest in the political sphere. We have already discussed the language-controls-thought theory as it appears in the writings of those involved in the arms control and defence community. Crypto-Whorfianism reaches the highest levels. On 29 October 1985 President Reagan told listeners to the British Radio 4 news programme, *The World At One* (a punning reference to pre-Babel unity that we generally do not notice), in reply to a question about the differences between,the US and the Soviet Union:

> Oh my heavens. Here are two systems so diametrically opposed that, I'm no linguist, but I've been told that in the Russian language there isn't even a word for freedom and two nations everyone's referring to as the Superpowers obviously are competitive and our philosophies and our ideas in the world, and that probably can't be corrected, but we can have a peaceful competition. (BBC transcript)

This text would certainly repay closer discourse analysis, but for now I merely want to mention the naive Whorfian theory lurking behind such remarks – or rather a kind of inverted Whorfianism, since it is being claimed here not that the *presence* of a lexical item determines the existence of certain characteristics of a world view, but that the *absence* of an item determines a conceptual *deficit*. This kind of implicit reasoning on Reagan's part may be no accident: a similarly crude brand of Whorfianism can sometimes be found in the literature of the strategic analysts, in which it has occasionally been argued that since Russian appears to have a lexical gap corresponding to the English word '*deterrence*', there is grave danger that they cannot be deterred![1] This is, of course, a fallacy that every first-year linguistics student could spot, but that doesn't exclude the possibility that it is ideologically persuasive in other quarters.

Herman Kahn, in *On Thermonuclear War* (1960), adopts an implicit theory of language, as well as assuming the ability – that is, the power – of the nuclear establishment to promote or impose a specially engineered variety of English to inculcate the nuclear truth (as seen by Kahn):

> One of the most important things that could be done to facilitate discussion of defense problems would be to create a vocabulary that is both small enough and simple enough to be learned, precise enough to communicate, and large enough so that all of the important ideas that are contending can be comfortably and easily described. One of my major objectives in writing this book is to facilitate the creation of such a vocabulary.

This is not so far removed from the utopian (or dystopian) language tradition; indeed, it is quite close to the linguistic fantasies of Orwell's Syme. The vocabulary of this Nukespeak is to be 'small enough' (Syme gloried in the destruction and reduction of words), 'precise', a container of specific ideas without vagueness or contention, a conduit capable of transmitting correct thoughts from one mind to another. The conception of language here is traditional and startlingly naive; but the power of the author to foster such ideas and to act upon them is deeply disturbing. Like the linguistic science fiction writers, Kahn is convinced language is all-important. Important it is, but if so, we must avoid giving it mythic proportions, and avoid basing our conclusions and our action on linguistic science fictions. In a sense Kahn has given the game away, for it would surely have been better from his point of view if the future consumers of his Nukespeak (for that is what he is outlining) did not believe that language mattered, were not conscious of its potential abuse. Often, in fact, politicians in power resist critiques of their linguistic trickery by accusing the critic of indulging in the vice of 'mere semantics'.

More subtly, Kahn is keenly aware of what we have called metaphor (including notions of frame, script, model, analogy and the like). Who now thinks of the term *escalation* ('laddering' in Anglo-Saxon English) as a metaphor? In *On Escalation: Metaphors and Scenarios* (1965), Kahn tells us that 'escalation is a relatively new word in the English language' (p. 3). And in following through this image of height, ascent, elevation, he notes: 'There are two interesting analogies or metaphors one can apply to escalation: the strike in labor disputes and the game of "chicken"' (p. 9). Indeed. It is not so much the word as the metaphorical 'application', the particular domains that are brought together. One may note in this connection that we have already encountered the metaphorical conflation of the domains of war, work and the schoolyard (Chapter 6). But what is even more important about Kahn's linguistics and language-engineering endeavours is the fact that his texts were powerful enough, given his status, connections and the reach of the publishing and educational institutions, to bring about the circulation of the term and concept *escalation*. The present currency of the term, and its particular uses, is evidence of that. In this instance, it seems reasonable to claim that with the word and its currently conventionalised use in political contexts goes an entire conceptual system for representing international relations and military strategy. Ironically, Kahn himself points out – disapprovingly – that metaphors can constrain thought (p. 9); it seems probable that this is precisely what has happened in this case, though not through the mere power of language, but rather through the power of the language user.[2]

A more recent example of pro-nuclear linguistic theorising that bears the hallmarks of the linguistic utopias and dystopias is contained in a tract entitled 'Semantics: USSR's Political Weapon', issued by the US Information Service (9 October 1985) and authored by Jim Guirard Jr., a Washington-based government consultant specialising in international security affairs. Once again there are the distinctive traits of the Newspeak grammarian's conception of language satirised by Orwell. Although it attacks the Soviet Union's supposed Orwellian Newspeak, it clearly takes seriously the absurd notion of language and communication that underlies 'Newspeak'. If we are to be serious and effective critics of language-use, it is important to escape from linguistic fictions and myths, as we have continually stressed. It is not surprising, in view of this, that Guirard's text is riddled with contradiction. It is based on, and legitimised by, claims attributed to a leading scholar of international affairs, Robert Tucker, and to George Richardson, chief executive officer of Oxford University Press, that the Soviet Union is busy 'transforming the world's dictionaries' as an 'ultimate weapon of political control'. This is a 'theft of language', where 'language' is apparently conceived as a pure vehicle of truth available to (Right-thinking) Americans. It is not just a matter of the Soviets changing the entries in their dictionaries, so that, for example, *capitalism* is defined as 'the system replacing feudalism and preceding communism'. According to Guirard, many people in the 'free world' have actually come to use English words with the meaning the Soviets have stipulated for them. It is not explained how the Soviets – or dictionaries, for that matter - are capable of achieving this extraordinary feat. 'Even now,' we are told, 'few in the West bother to use the term 'liberation' for what President Reagan achieved in Grenada in late 1983. Nor are communist assassination teams labelled as the left-wing death squads they really are – nor is the anti-communist struggle in Nicaragua called the 'New Revolution' it really is'. No ambivalence about the action in Grenada is allowed, no contention about the vocabulary appropriate to describe it. Word and thing are thought by Guirard to go together in a natural signifying unity: Reagan's action was a 'liberation'; any other term is a distortion of this Platonic truth. Linguistic skullduggery there certainly is, at all points in the political spectrum. But it is interesting that it is largely on the Right that public effort is made to bolster language manipulation with spurious linguistic science fiction. There are two major misconceptions in Guirard's text. First, dictionaries simply do not have the power to globally prescribe meaning and use in the way he claims. Second, there is a quaintly Platonic or pre-Babelic conception of meaning underlying the notion that a thing can be truly described as it 'really is' by the application of some naturally given 'label'. Apparently, only 'the West' knows what real reality is, and has the right set of linguistic labels to affix to its contents. It is presumably on this basis that in 1985 the US Advisory Commission on Public Diplomacy strongly recommended that the National Security Council establish a task force (yes, a Task Force!) 'to assess the problem of semantics in the international "war of words" and propose an institutionalised political discourse'. At least Orwell's Syme had a cynical awareness that Newspeak was intended to define reality in the state's interest. The last example of entrenched and misleading conceptions of language is derived from a base metaphor with serious, perhaps deleterious, implications for international relations. It will receive focal attention, since it makes more substantial scientific claims, and also has at least some positive contribution to make to our understanding of what is going on in the discourse between the superpowers. It is a paper by Dr Coral Bell, formerly Professor of International Relations at the University of Sussex and a specialist in crisis analysis. The model of language selected here (and, as we have argued, one's choice or construction of a linguistic model in general can have ideological motivation and/or effects) is not Whorfian and culture-based. Rather, as you might guess from the title (and, by an odd coincidence, perhaps from the author's name), it is based on a communications-engineering metaphor. It is this and its implications that I want to examine critically, but before launching into that it is important to review and assess the types of language-related work that have been produced by the proponents of peace and conflict studies.

One such area is the American School of 'General Semantics', going back to Korzybski and to Hayakawa, but still represented in a recent paper by the mathematician and games-theorist Anatol Rapoport.[3] The main limitation of this kind of work, to my mind, is its notion of language as a 'conceptual map'. This model of language appears to neglect the pragmatic dimension (that is, in general, the role of context, social structure and the distribution of power). It tends to reify language, and to underestimate the fact that language can also be action. The psycholinguistic work of Charles Osgood is also somewhat in this tradition, although his adaptation of cognitive dissonance ('try to be or seem consistent') theory and the Pollyanna ('Look on the bright side') principle does have pragmatic implications and, specifically, pragmatic implications for the reciprocal reduction of international tension.[4]

Another area is the more recent work in Europe, especially in Belgium, Holland and Germany (which now has a 'Wissenschaftler für den Frieden' group), and to some extent in France. Much of this work has been intentionally polemical, my own included, though the move is now towards more detailed theorisation – as is reflected in Fritz Pasierbsky's *Krieg and Frieden in der Sprache* (Fischer, 1983), which gives a large place to (informal) pragmatics and to discourse analysis.

What is lacking from both these areas of work is input from the political scientists and their understanding of the 'international context'. This is surely required for an applied political pragmatics of the type that may be emerging. This is not to say that political scientists themselves have been inactive, and in particular I want to mention and make use of Franck and Weisband's *Word Politics*. The book came out in 1972 and has since been overtaken, first by the collapse of détente and then by the Gorbachev thaw. But its interest lies in the fact that it analyses some of the same events as Coral Bell, but from a quite different political (and linguistic) perspective from the one she promotes. And, more to the point for our purposes, it does so in terms translatable into the central notions of the pragmatics of language. Although Franck and Weisband do not refer to Austin, Grice and Searle, they adopt the formal principle that the word/act distinction is invalid. They also set up a 'principle of reciprocity' for international relations, which is not unlike the (to linguists) more familiar 'Co-operative Principle' developed by the philosopher Paul Grice and widely adopted by researchers working in the field of the pragmatics of language. The 'Co-operative Principle', which has some similarity to Habermas's validity claims, says that communication works because speakers and hearers rationally co-operate in mutually expecting one another to be truthful, to be just sufficiently informative and to be clear. And they closely examine 'verbal acts', which they call 'enunciations' (like 'declaratives'), and 'offers', which they treat partly in an ethnographic fashion.

What I am arguing towards is a confrontation of two linguistic approaches towards international relations: Coral Bell's, on the one hand, and one based on pragmatics on the other. I shall now try to give a brief description and critique of Bell's theory, and in so doing I shall imply not merely that an applied pragmatics approach yields an analysis that is politically more congenial to me personally, but also that it gives a better account of the facts of communicative phenomena. I shall then conclude by trying to indicate some ways in which the applied pragmatics of international communication might be further explored.

The Bell approach can be summarised by means of the following diagram:

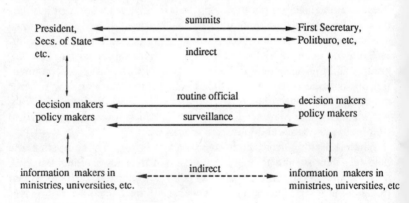

This is not Bell's own diagram, but it is based on her description. At first glance, it has some merits: it gives some idea of the complexity of the process; secondly, it incorporates non-verbal as well as verbal 'signals', and, thirdly, it apparently allows for 'distortion' of 'messages' up and down a power pyramid on either side. There are, however, a number of possible criticisms. The first is that the existence of the rest of the population, and the relationship between it and the power pyramids, is not included. The reason for this emerges from Bell's discussion of what she calls 'Asymmetry in Communication-Flow'. By this she means that the Soviet Union 'emits' less information to the United States, and in general talks less, than the Americans do; and she explains this by pointing out that the Soviet Union censors and controls the information-flow to its own people, while claiming that the United States does not.

The differences between the two states and their social regimes are undeniable and not trivial. But Bell's account leaves the nature of public discourse in the West unanalysed. It assumes not only that people have free access to information (which is legally true, of course, in the US under the Freedom of Information Act), but also that people have equal rights to speak and be heard. This is almost certainly not the case, and it is incidentally one of the defects of certain types of discourse and pragmatic analysis that they tend to neglect the fact that speakers do not have equal rights to issue 'felicitous' (i.e. functional and acceptable) requests, objections, warnings, offers and so forth.[5]

This is, of course, a consequence of our particular social arrangements, not of language viewed as an abstract system; but in so far as pragmatics and discourse analysis are concerned with the interaction between language and social processes, they need, in my view, to take into account the unequal distribution of power in institutionalised communication settings. This point applies on both a small and large scale. On the small scale, asymmetrical power will determine rights to certain kinds of illocutionary force in, for example, doctor-patient settings, pupil–teacher discourse and male–female encounters; and it will affect politeness phenomena, as is well known. But, on the large scale of public discourse as mediated by television, radio, newspapers, official publications and so forth, we need also to think in terms of limitations on rights to take turns, rights to issue information, express attitudes, challenge assertions, and so on. That is to say, it is quite reasonable to point out that public relations and information management, for instance, remain the preserve of certain groups of people.

A particular case of the communicational power possessed by certain groups in Western societies is the power to bring about the circulation of lexical material, in particular euphemisms and metaphors which ultimately have an ideological function. This fact, if accepted as such, is relevant to criticisms of Soviet information management, though the latter in themselves are no doubt justified. Bell argues, for instance, that the Russians have a strategic advantage in controlling information flow to their own people about repression in Afghanistan, whereas such control was not possible for the Americans in Vietnam. What this claim neglects is that the United States bureaucracy (as well as the Soviet Union) was able, to a degree at least, to manage attitudes and perceptions by means of the dissemination (inter alia) of euphemisms like 'surgical strike', 'protective reaction', 'P.R. strikes', 'suppressive fire' and 'aggressive defense'. The term 'protective reaction' was first used on 9 October 1969 by Secretary of Defence Melvin Laird: the point is that the 'coining' of such phrases requires peculiar contextual factors that involve authority and access to media as necessary conditions. If we accept some degree of skewing of discursive power *within* Western societies, then it needs to be included in Bell's picture, for there are two consequences for the discourse between the superpowers. One is that the population does not (contrary to the claims of certain analysts) wholly govern the discourse between them – as indeed Bell's own inclusion of a 'filter' that distorts information should imply; and the other is that since the bystanding, 'overhearing' public cannot wholly influence the course of the 'conversation', that 'conversation' may need to be rhetorically managed, presented, packaged in such a way as to maintain the public's support. The public is, of course, intended to 'overhear', but it is not necessarily the case that it is intended to know that it is intended to 'overhear'.

I want to turn now to a second and more fundamental objection to Bell's model. This is that it rests, implicitly, on what Reddy has called a 'conduit' or, to use Roy Harris's term, 'telementational' conception of communication.[6] That is to say, it seems to assume that discrete, determinate messages 'flow' along channels from one receptacle to another, one mind to another. The messages may be 'amplified' or 'faint' or suffer 'interference' from 'noise' or 'static', but despite the information interpreters on the diagram, no real account is taken either of inferential work in the comprehension and production of meaning or of interpersonal meaning and its indeterminacies. The conception of language with which Bell is working appears to be derived rather narrowly from the information theory of the 1940s – narrowly, because the notion of message here is conflated with that of signal, which it is not in the most thorough early work, where *signals* are transmitted, while receivers *construe* the *messages* from these signals with the aid of contextual and other evidence. In the narrow interpretation of the theory, which is telementational, interpretations are somehow seen as *contained* in the signal. Reddy believes that the mathematical basis of information theory was subtle enough to reflect the true nature of the communication process, but that the pervasive conduit metaphor constrained popularised versions of the theory, so that scientific credence was given to traditional conceptions of thoughts packed into code and subsequently unpacked by a receiving mind without indeterminacy or interpretive interaction. This is a mythical view of language, a fantasy of pure communication before the tower of Babel. It is a broadcasting tower concept of communication, curiously mirrored in the diagram we have derived from Bell's description.

Bell and other strategic analysts seem to assume that arms deployments work in this straightforward signalling fashion. For them, nuclear weapons send unequivocal 'signals' containing unequivocal 'messages' ('We are strong', and the like). But the evidence is that the Soviet Union will not always, as the phrase goes, get the message. Rather they may work out a quite different meaning, drawing on contextual and background information (including, for instance, the history of invasion of their territory by West European powers), that the US is threatening or coercing. Similarly, the US analysts are not necessarily 'receiving' the correct message in applying their (implicit) theory of signals transmission to Soviet actions.

This is a complex and subtle area, and one which requires careful semiotic and linguistic investigation. All I am suggesting is that, instead of the communications engineering model, we should adopt the different and more plausible metaphor of two (perhaps three) *people* in conversational interaction. There is clearly a risk of oversimplification here, but it is at least in line with our metaphorical way of referring to the two superpower blocs 'talking to one another','engaging in dialogue', etc. This proposal clearly requires further justification. But it is worth noting, in addition, that the pragmatics of communication is about the construction of meaning, and that this is likely to be applicable in any activity requiring construal of a signal from a human source.

Let us compare the two approaches as they have been applied to a particular historical case of superpower confrontation. Bell offers an analysis of the classic Cuban missile crisis based on her communication model. Specifically, she seeks to explain both the cause and the resolution of the conflict by referring to three features of this model namely (i) the 'multi-channelled' structure, (ii) 'strength of signal', and (iii) 'feedback'. She gives us the following causal sequence of events (here simplified slightly, with the crucial communicative acts in italics):

> Abortive American invasion at Bay of Pigs; warnings from the US not heeded; this automatically signals 'we aren't tough', so when Castro requests Soviet security, the Soviet Union *agrees* and attacks US. Kennedy goes on TV and issues a *warning*, *committing* himself thereby to his position of meeting force with force by means of a blockade.
>
> Soviet Union uses various channels to *reply*. Another 'crucial signal' is an article in an American newspaper *suggesting* that American Thor and Jupiter missiles stationed in Turkey might be traded in. In the next stage, this 'signal' reaches Soviet Union and becomes 'feedback' facilitating a settlement...

I am not able to judge the historical accuracy of this account; it is, in particular, unclear whether the Russians were aware of and took into account the possibility of a *quid pro quo* on Thor and Jupiter, but some linguistic observations are in order. First, the supposed 'signal' from the Bay of Pigs is *unexplained*: it is presented as a simple unitary and determinate 'emission'. Secondly, what Bell refers to as a 'strong signal' – that is, Kennedy's crucial TV appearance – can be more fully analysed as a crucial conventional verbal act (or 'illocutionary act', as speech act theory terms it): namely, at least one kind of *warning* (of a blockade) and what we can term an *engagement* (I have italicised other relevant speech act verbs). This 'engagement', which accounts for what Bell calls the '*strength* of the signal', depends, in pragmatic terms, on 'mutual knowledge'. Although the concept of mutual knowledge has taken a back seat in recent pragmatics theorising, it can usefully be rehabilitated; in particular it is needed for a linguistic understanding of certain kinds of political discourse, the prime case being the discourse of *deterrence*. In the Cuba case, and perhaps in others, we need to extend the mutual knowledge principle to include not only the speaker and the hearer, but also the overhearer. That is, the speaker (S) knows that the hearer (H) knows that S ... knows that the United States will blockade; and, in addition, S knows that the audience knows that H knows, etc. This basis for international 'comprehension' then needs to be related to the speech acts constitutive of this piece of international 'discourse'.

My third point about Bell's account of the Cuban crisis concerns the idea of 'feedback', which seems simply imposed on the data by the model, since it appears on the face of it unlikely that the Soviets needed the American press to tell them about the American missiles in Turkey, and unlikely that they were incapable of making the proposals without the supposed 'signal' from the newspaper columnist. It is by no means clear from Bell's account how the Thor and Jupiter entered into the eventual settlement, if they did at all.

Franck and Weisband give the Thor missiles a quite different role in their account of the Cuba crisis, an account which I take to be more compatible with a pragmatics-based account of international discourse. Their analysis extends the context and includes an earlier event, the American intervention in Guatemala in 1954, and is on the whole more *explanatory*, in the sense that it does not assume unitary, determinate 'signals', but depends on interaction between rational agents drawing inferences from declared principles in conjunction with physical 'gestures'; it also incorporates an illocutionary analysis, although it does not explicitly refer to it in those terms. In the summary below I gloss Franck and Weisband's analysis in order to bring out potential pragmatic explanations.

The US intervenes in Guatemala and in various forums *publicly declares* the right of America to do so in the region as a defence against 'international communism' [i.e. there was a series of specific performative acts dependent on specific institutionalized conditions, and in general much discursive work went into legitimating American control of wayward neighbours.]

The Bay of Pigs intervention was then consistent with these principles, although abortive. Continuing the summary,

> Castro *infers* that American intervention is again likely, on the basis of the earlier official utterances and actions (i.e. he assumes some kind of 'conversational' principle of consistency or relevance). Kennedy *commits* himself to his *warnings*, by choosing a specific medium and timing. But the Soviets persist (that is, the *warning* does not have the desired perlocutionary effect). The reason suggested by Franck and Weisband is that the Soviets *inferred* that the Thor Missiles in Turkey legitimated Soviet missiles in Cuba.

In other words according to Franck and Weisband, the missiles stationed in Turkey were a contributory causal factor in the initiation of the crisis, not (as Bell claims) an element of its resolution. Franck and Weisband, like Bell, believe Kennedy did not know the missiles were still there, thought this is probably an incorrect assumption. The point for Franck and Weisband, however, is that Kennedy could (or, as we now perhaps ought to say, should) have invoked a 'reciprocal proscriptive principle' on border missile deployments. The fact that he did not do so explains, in their account, the origin and deepening of the crisis (though not, of course, its eventual resolution). In the event, Soviet face was saved by the American guarantee never to invade Cuba, and the missiles were 'in return' withdrawn. Franck and Weisband's version can be looked at in the light of something like Grice's cooperative principles. Consider the two last phases of the episode listed above. According to the Gricean Maxim of Quantity (Give the right amount of information), Kennedy might have been expected to speak to justify the presence of US missiles in Turkey. But he didn't; consequently the Soviets accepted a political *implicature* from Kennedy's *silence* to the effect that superpowers can legitimately park missiles in one another's backyards. Franck and Weisband's account depends, broadly, on two factors: first, the communicative reasoning of rational agents, and second, the dependence of such reasoning on what they call the 'reciprocity principle'. These parameters of international communication could, I think, be seen as analogous to the co-operative principle and conversational implicatures of conventional pragmatics. This particular analysis may or may not be historically correct. My point is to illustrate how a pragmatics-based approach may be applied, and applied more coherently, to conflict scenarios than the information signal model of Bell.

Finally, I want to sketch out some ways of looking at the pragmatics of *offers*, which I take to be central in arms race negotiations, in particular the so-called 'zero option' of 1981 on Euromissiles and Soviet SS20s, and the later so-called 'offer' on SDI. Earlier I said that in a three-participant communication system (with a notional *speaker*, *hearer*, and *audience*) such as international communication is, we need to take account of the superpowers' 'presentation' to their publics of their 'conversation'. What I shall suggest is that performative verbs such as *offer* are used to refer, misleadingly, to illocutions that are not pragmatically viable as offers, or are in some way in bad faith or dominating, that is to say, ideologically motivated.

There is more than one linguistically interesting feature of the discourse of the 'zero-option' period, but we will focus on the supposed 'offer' itself, and also abstract it drastically from its contemporary textual setting. Let us assume it can be stated as a conditional: *If you withdraw your SS20s, we will not deploy cruise and Pershing II*.

For such an utterance to be effectively performed, we have first to assume at least three conditions: namely, that the performer is a duly authorised individual, that s/he is speaking in a duly authorised setting, and that s/he has the capability to bring about the state of affairs offered. These conditions are not sufficient, since for the utterance to be taken as an offer, the benefit to the hearer has to be maximised, the cost of the condition minimised.[7] That was, of course, by no means obvious to the hearer (the Soviet Union) at the time, or even to the overhearer (some of the Western public), and so led to further linguistic manipulations on the definition of classes of weapons systems, which we need not go into.[8] But even if the cost/benefit ratio to the hearer and speaker were clear, there is something distinctly odd about 'offering' *not* to do something. It is so odd that non-conditional negative offers appear as ungrammatical. One cannot say '(Do) let me *not* hit you over the head (for you)' and be making an offer comparable to '(Do) let me carry your bags (for you)'. The functional pragmatic reason for this would presumably be that such 'offers' implicate a positive intention to commit a harmful act, which is being denied.[9] Not surprisingly, the logically equivalent form of the proposal, in which the 'offer' part is positive, has a different illocutionary force from its negative counterpart: 'If you do not withdraw your SS20s, we will deploy Cruise and Pershing,' which is prima facie a *threat*. There is clearly more to say about the pragmatics of threats and offers. But two points arise from this example. One is that a *genuine* conditional offer was pragmatically impossible at the time. The other is that maybe certain kinds of (positive) non-conditional (i.e. unilateral) offers stand a better chance of working, since the cost to the hearer is not specified.

However, these, too, have to fulfil certain delicate requirements, as the peculiar case of the apparently unilateral SDI or Star Wars 'offer' of late 1985 suggests. In this case, I shall refer to an attested text, and in so doing draw attention to other discourse factors. This text is one of several in which the so-called offer has been made in recent months:

Widlake: But the Russians presumably would have to make their own SDI? You wouldn't offer it to them, would you, off the shelf?

Reagan: Why not? And I think this is something to be discussed at the summit as to what kind of agreement we could make in the event. I would like to say to the Soviet Union: We know you have been researching for this same thing longer than we have. We wish you well. There couldn't be anything better than if both of us came up with it, but if only one of us does, then why don't we, instead of using it as an offensive means of having a first strike against anyone else in the world, why don't we use it to ensure that there won't be any nuclear strikes?

Widlake: Are you saying then, Mr President, that the United States, if it were well down the road towards a proper SDI programme, would be prepared to share its technology with Soviet Russia, provided of course there were arms reductions and so on, on both sides?

Widlake's question actually invites President Reagan to confirm or agree to a negative proposition, namely, that he would *not* 'offer' SDI to the Russians 'off the shelf'. I think it can be assumed that the function of the phrase *off the shelf* is, here, to minimise the apparent cost to the potential beneficiary. Reagan does not, however, confirm or agree. He replies to the question with another question: why not? – that is to say, he asks Widlake for reasons. Now this is a rhetorical question: it expects no answer. And the reason is that the discourse-setting conventions, together with the status differential of the participants, preclude Widlake's giving reasons. Widlake and Reagan know this; nonetheless, via the Maxim of Quantity ('give as much information as is required'), it is implicated (at least for the overhearer) that there are no reasons, and thus that SDI would be 'offered off the shelf'. It is important to note, however, that the co-operative principle alone is insufficient: power relations of some sort block a reply and get the question interpreted precisely as 'rhetorical'. The reasons for the interactive indirectness is plain: the 'offer' is *not* wholly 'off the shelf' or without cost, or even cheap at the price, as the subsequent text (and background knowledge, of course) indicates. This is, then, not a unilateral offer, though it may seem like it. Even if it were (that is, even if it *were* beneficial), however, there are plausible pragmatic reasons, derived this time from Politeness (or Diplomatic?) Principles, why this 'offer' might be pragmatically infelicitous.[10] Politeness Principles include, to borrow from Geoffrey Leech's work, a 'Generosity Maxim' that minimises *cost* to self and a 'Modesty Maxim' that minimises *praise* of self. The SDI offer, both in referential substance and in the way the texts express it, would probably infringe both. Franck and Weisband remind us that in many cultures elaborate rituals exist to minimise the cost to the giver of a gift, and to prepare the act itself.[11] The pragmatic reasoning behind these restraints is that the greater the offer, the greater the power and prestige of the offerer; and the greater the obligation of the recipient to reciprocate. This implies that even an unconditional SDI offer is an expression of power, and one that cannot be reciprocated, though it remains one that can always be *presented* as a genuine offer, while the refusing side can be presented as ungracious or irrational. The lesson is that offers need to be initially small and capable of reciprocation, if a process is to be set in motion. In fact, this is the conclusion that is built into Osgood's theory of reciprocal tension reduction. It now seems possible to explicate Osgood's proposals in the light of linguistic pragmatics – a body of research not available to him at the time, but surely consistent with his concern for the linguistic aspects of international communication.

Let me sum up by making three broad points. First, there is scope for linguists to join political and strategic analysts in criticising and elucidating verbal interaction between superpowers. Secondly, in such an enterprise the choice of linguistic model is crucial – and likely to involve ideological motivations. Thirdly, there seems to be scope for the exploration of an applied pragmatics of international discourse. There remains, of course, major theoretical and practical problems which I've done no more than sketch in the barest outline.

Nukespeak
Chasing its Tail

1. Cultural Recycling

The foregoing attempt to make sense of the ways in which language is used and has been used in relation to the problems of the nuclear age advanced on two broad fronts. First, I have raised the question of the 'origin' of nukespeak, both in a psychological sense (why do we need it and what does it do to our minds?), and in a historical and social-political sense (who produces it and who consumes it?). Secondly, I have tried to indicate certain linguistic processes that may operate in (but are not necessarily unique to) the subvariety of English used in discourse about nuclear weapons and nuclear policy.

With respect to the first point, there is evidence that 'nukespeak' spreads outwards from official sources via the media to the consuming public. It is fairly clear, for instance, that in August 1945 a certain style emerged for referring to the three atomic bombs that were exploded, and that this style spread from the scientists immediately concerned with the tests and the bombings to the political mouthpieces and then to the newspapers. We do not know how much of it entered public discourse, or how much it influenced the public mind, although letters back to major newspapers do suggest that the style was received and utilised. However, it would be over-simple to think of the propagation of nuclear language as a one-way process of imposition: the theory of nukespeak is not a conspiracy theory but a complicity theory. The need to assimilate the experience of the bomb was general, as was the need for a 'language' to handle the experience.

To turn to the second issue of linguistic processes, two main areas of language use are important. The first concerns syntax: though many of the manipulations considered are found in all areas of persuasive or coercive interaction, there is one fairly common syntactic tendency that is peculiarly significant in the present context. This is the choice of constructions that evade overt reference to human agency and/or intentionality, and which often ascribe agency and intentionality, either explicitly or implicitly, to non-human entities. This practice tallies with the most prominent feature of nuclear language – the production of semantic shifts to refer to new phenomena. The most interesting of such shifts are metaphors (whether in the form of metaphor proper, nicknames or extended 'arguments'). Many of the metaphors involved derive from deeply rooted traditions that seem to have a primitive hold on the human mind. To this extent, the emergence of 'nukespeak' is irrational, and its continuation is irrational. Now that we have considered some characteristics of nuclear language, it might be worthwhile looking, albeit in a highly speculative fashion, for further explanations both of its origins and of its evident grip on the imagination.

The 'complicity theory' of nukespeak assumes that there was a mass need, both for a way of representing a new physical experience and for easing guilt and fear. The one need is cognitive and conceptual, the other interpersonal and emotional. They are not independent, however, and a solution to one could be a solution to the other.

Broadly speaking, human culture does not cope with the new by means of new terms, new symbols, new images. It seeks to familiarise the new by using old terms, symbols and images in slightly different ways. The question, then, is: What images were there in our culture that could be recycled to tame and make sense of what was an undoubtedly overwhelming new experience? We have long had symbols for handling experience of *natural* phenomena that are gigantic, violent and destructive – phenomena such as thunder, lightning, eruptions and floods. Confronted with such things, humans have (a) categorised them as supernatural, and (b) projected their own intentionality on to them. In general terms it is *animism* – the projection of agency and intentionality on to nature – that made it possible, early in the evolution of human culture, to confront both harmful and harmless physical events. The biologist Jacques Monod states it thus:

> Animist belief ... consists essentially in a projection into inanimate nature of man's awareness of the intensely teleonomic functioning of his own central nervous system. It is, in other words, the hypothesis that natural phenomena can and must be explained in the same manner...as subjective human activity. Primitive animism formulated this hypothesis with complete candour, frankness and precision, populating nature with gracious or awe-inspiring myths and myth-figures which for centuries nourished art and poetry.[1]

As we have seen in examining the reaction of scientists to 'Trinity', and in examining the names of the weapons systems themselves, these myths and myth-figures also nourish politics and military planning. But there is something odd, something different, in this recycling of images from what has happened in previous eras of human culture. In the nuclear period, the 'natural phenomena' are products of culture itself; the titanic violence is not produced by nature, but by man. Whereas in earlier periods culture projected itself into nature, culture now projects itself into itself, culture into culture, for the bomb is the product of human culture:

$$\text{culture} \longrightarrow \text{nature}$$
$$\downarrow$$
$$\text{culture} \longrightarrow \text{culture}$$

Instead of giving god-like properties to natural events, we now ascribe god-like properties to human artifacts.[2] This transformation has some serious consequences. It is not just a case of the 'culture–culture' relation replacing the earlier one, but of the two being in some sense superimposed. If this is so, then there are two effects. First, human culture (that is, the technological culture of our time) is recategorised as 'natural', and consequently endowed with its own agency and purposiveness beyond human control. We have seen many examples of this above, both in grammar and vocabulary. Secondly, since it is *human* culture that is 'naturalised', humans themselves are categorised as elements of nature beyond control – their own control. This is paradoxical and contradictory: that is the reason why it is compelling, but also the reason why it cannot be sustained much longer. The cultural recycling can be summarised thus: culture projects itself into nature; culturised nature projects itself into culture:

$$\text{culture} \longrightarrow \begin{array}{l}\textbf{culturised}\\ \textbf{nature}\end{array}$$

E.P. Thompson has spoken of the 'hideous cultural abnormalities' of the nuclear age. It is these 'abnormalities' that surmount, in a fashion, the problem of incomprehension, which has been stated in the following way by Nicholas Humphrey:

> I do not see how any human being whose intelligence and sensitivities have been shaped by traditional facts and values could possibly understand the nature of these unnatural, otherworldly weapons...Our minds are finely tuned by culture and by evolution to respond to the frequencies of the real world. And when an alien message comes through on an alien wavelength it sets up no vibrations.[3]

This account states the permanent and limiting effect of human culture, and the enormity of the problem when human culture confronts something outside its existing paradigms. However, since culture is adaptive and dynamic, it does not just switch off or go on to another wavelength (though that is one course of action), but it reinterprets the incoming signals in its own terms. The weapons are – *prior* to culturisation – 'unnatural' and 'otherworldly'; but they become 'natural' *after* assimilation, even if they retain their 'otherworldly' aura.

This approach might be taken in conjunction with Mandelbaum's account of the 'cultural restraints' affecting chemical and nuclear weapons.[4] He asks why chemical weapons have apparently been more successfully (although not entirely) outlawed and tabooed than nuclear weapons. One of his explanations is that restraints on chemical weapons are 'deeply and broadly based in human culture, and may be related to taboos that serve the basic human need of ordering the universe, of drawing boundaries for human activity'. Chemical weapons, one may suppose, transgress such basic cultural boundaries as healing and death, war and peace. (It may also be worth pointing out that *gas* derives etymologically from *chaos*.) Another explanation is that aversion to toxic substances is crucial in evolutionary terms, and may be genetically coded. He also points out that it is culturally coded in the universally abhorred myth-figure of the poisoner. By contrast, 'explosions are of more much recent provenance', and it seems unlikely that human evolution would have been affected by them in the same degree. To Mandelbaum's arguments we can add that explosions – natural ones in the first instance – are actually coded positively, if ambivalently, in many myths and religions, in the form of thunder gods, sun gods and the like. Further, human explosions – from gunpowder explosions on – are already coded in the same terms (by the cultural recycling process). And nuclear explosions though physically of a different and strictly incomprehensible order, are slotted into the same paradigm.

This is a dangerous process for *Homo sapiens*. The work of Jacques Monod enables us to grasp the nature of the problem and the kind of resolution it might have. What we have seen, at least in part, is the spread of a mythic solution at a critical moment in human culture. The 'spreading power' of an idea, claims Monod, 'depends upon pre-existing structures in the mind, among them ideas already implanted by culture, but also undoubtedly upon certain innate structures which are very difficult for us to identify.'[5] These pre-existing structures, Monod suggests, require a global explanation that places human beings in a scheme of things and thereby relieves their anxiety in a hostile universe. But, he goes on, the emergence of science in human history, by contradicting the old animist harmony of man and nature, has produced a 'sickness of the spirit' and a sense of helplessness. And it is the nuclear age that he links with this sickness:

> All this – the spirit's disorder and the nuclear stockpile alike – comes from one simple idea: that nature is objective, that the systematic confrontation of logic and experience is the sole source of true knowledge.[6]

The nuclear stockpile has come from the development of science, but so has the human helplessness that stems from the intellectual unacceptability of the old mythic structures. What the evidence of nuclear language suggests is that the sickness has been so severe in the face of nuclear explosions that the human brain has actually returned to the old structures in order, contradictorily, to explain that which undermines them. This is precisely the conflict that Monod sees in contemporary societies. While science has been granted a prestigious place, it has not removed the animistic structures that, in Monod's view, still underlie modern ideologies, whether Western 'liberal' ideologies or Marxist ones based on the 'materialist and dialectical religion of history.'[7]

2. The Strange Loop Syndrome

Monod's theory of a (possibly genetically endowed) need for mythic explanation can help us understand the apparent acceptability of nuclear weapons. For they can be reinterpreted in terms which answer a deep-seated human need. It has often been noticed that nuclear weapons are not merely *acceptable* to many people, they actually exert a peculiar, morbid fascination, as Dr Strangelove found. One reason for this is the nature of the mythic schema in which the bomb is caught up. Mythic schemas – the Christian one is a good example – make evil, suffering and death not only acceptable but *desirable*. They are part of a universal scheme of things that has to be desirable because it *is*. Suffering and death are supposed to be followed by – indeed they are the only route to – Resurrection and the Apocalypse, the eradication of all things that is at the same time the revelation of all things. There are born-again Christians who teach that the nuclear holocaust (a holocaust is a totally burnt offering to God) is the fulfilment of biblical texts. I have heard Anglican parsons hint at the same thing. Whether these mythic structures are set in our chromosomes or in our cultural traditions or both, they help to explain our macabre fascination with nuclear apocalyptics. But notice that all these structures depend on paradox and ambivalence of one kind and another whose function is to resolve primal contradictions. It is by focussing on this aspect that I want to approach the nature of nuclear fascination.

> We have gone on piling weapon upon weapon, missile upon missile ... like the victims of some sort of hypnotism, like men in a dream, like lemmings heading for the sea.

Another image that has been used is the image of the rabbit fascinated by the twisting snake.[8] This is a mixed bag of powerful analogies that have a ring of truth when applied to our own situation. However, how appropriate is it to use analogies taken from animal behaviour? Animal behaviour is largely genetically transmitted. Human behaviour has a much larger cultural component, though that does not rule out an inherited capacity for culture or even an inherited capacity to structure it in specific ways. The capacity for language is the most obvious and spectacular aspect of human culture, and the aspect that distinguishes human behaviour most sharply. Lemmings and rabbits, presumably, are genetically predetermined to 'permit' their own destruction. So may humans be – *but* it is at least as likely that any urge to self-destruction they have is embodied more in their culture and less in their genes. Rabbits mesmerised by the twisting snake are, moreover, mesmerised by a visual stimulus. Now, few people have actually seen an atomic detonation; yet it still rings true intuitively to speak of people being mesmerised by the idea, if not by the physical stimulus. The scientists and the politicians who reacted to the Alamogordo explosion did not record a 'primitive' response, like the rabbit recording its reaction to the stimulus in its immobility. The human reaction was immediately to *interpret* the explosion in cultural terms, through the medium of language. I want to suggest further that, for example, it is not that the word 'Trinity' referred to (the test) but the *concept* which fascinates the mind, as it always has done. How can this and other images and arguments work?

The image of the mesmerised rabbit and the image of hypnosis are perhaps a clue. The rabbit is mesmerised by the spiral of a twisting snake. And, curiously enough, photographic images of the mushroom cloud of atomic and nuclear explosions show clearly their spiral form. Humans can be hypnotised by circular motion. The circle is, too, a widespread mystical symbol which is held to absorb the mind. There may be a neurological explanation for such reactions. However, for the present argument the relevant feature is the fascinating effect of oscillatory and circular motion. Another phenomenon which appears to have a hypnotic effect on the human brain is the optical illusion. These are especially interesting because they produce their effect by offering contradictory information to the visual centres, with the result that the brain oscillates between alternative interpretations of the image. But these examples involve direct sensory stimulation. The bomb does not itself affect brains in that direct way. In what ways could images of it and arguments about it affect the brain analogously?

I have already referred to paradox and spiral in connection with hypnotic effects. As it happens, these are important terms in the language of nuclear discussion. We are told that deterrence is a 'paradox', and sometimes that we should try to understand it and accept it (believe it, like the Trinity, even if you cannot make sense of it, urge the nuclear high-priests). The arms race is referred to as a 'spiral', usually by those who reject it, since spirals appear to perpetuate a circular motion in space, and arms races –

at least the nuclear one – appear to perpetuate a circular process in time. The term 'escalation' captures a similar idea. The use of such words reflects an awareness of the nature of the things they refer to, but they do not immediately reveal the pervasive hold over the human mind which paradoxes, spirals and circles can have.[9]

The arms race and the military–industrial interaction in weapons development are material historical cycles taking place through time. The logic of mutual deterrence may also be, or may also have been, a material historical circle in human behaviour. You can't see them directly, as the rabbit sees the twisting snake, but you do perhaps internalise them in various ways, including verbal ways. To talk of arms spirals and logics of deterrence is already to verbalise, conceptualise and in all probability reduce what is complex (and seems messy) to an order that suits pre-existing patterns of the human brain. Spirals, loops and circles are possibly patterns that the brain finds pleasing, and hypnotic – dangerously so, at the present stage of human culture. There is a gulf between the reality of our actions and the ways we want to represent them to ourselves, and to become ensnared in our mental representations is the greatest paradox of all, the most dangerous, since it can generate self-destruction.

3. A 'Grammar' for the Arms Race and Other Spirals

How do we picture the arms spiral? Here is one way of representing graphically and schematically an arms contest through time. (The time axis is arbitrary, but assumes a starting point where one of the two contestants [] and O acquires nuclear arms. The other axis assumes we can assign a measure to the quantity and quality of weapons.)

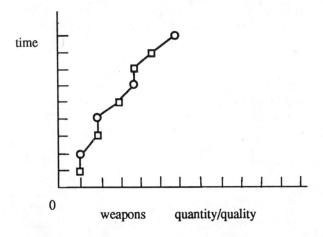

Notice that, once parity is achieved, either side may move to superiority first; once one side has superiority, the other side may decide to catch up, or skip a stage and leapfrog. As it becomes possible to predict stages in technological development, so the temptation to anticipate and outpace the adversary may increase. This is a crude picture of the two sides' 'performance' in practice. It appears open-ended. It appears self-contained. And it does not represent the dynamic driving force that generates the spiral. We might think of the driving force as a 'grammar', a set of 'moves' that tell you the form of possible outputs or actions. (Languages are highly complex sets of 'rules', i.e. grammars, that interact to specify the form of acceptable structures.)

Let's assume, for the sake of simplicity, that there are two sides, a and b, who can move in three ways: they can 'perceive' one another (a perceives b); a can catch up with b ($a = b$) and a can go to the next stage ahead of b ($a = b + 1$). We can then make a simple 'grammar' like this, allowing a to start the system off with $a = 1$:

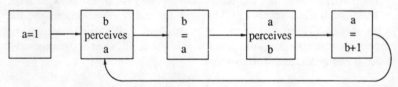

To represent an arms race where the sides skip stages, etc., we would need a more complicated 'grammar', but the crucial thing – the strange loop that brings us back to where we started – remains, and so do the 'perceives' boxes, which are actually the most crucial of all.

What is the status of such pictures? They are clearly grotesquely inadequate. For a start, they exclude interaction with other systems. The term 'perceives' glosses over a complex process of assessing 'threats' and seeking 'superiority'. They assume, moreover, that the system is indefinitely self-perpetuating. It has indeed been argued that the arms race loop is self-perpetuating precisely because of the nature of nuclear arms – they cannot be used, so the present arms race loop cannot be stopped in the way previous arms races have been stopped: by the outbreak of war.[10] However, the factor which complicates this fascinating spiral most dangerously is the desire to escape from it by inventing weapons which *can* be used, or which people believe to be usable. Such pictures are thus highly misleading and dangerous, but they do seem to underlie the arguments that are put forward by nuclear apologists. The 'moves' of the above 'grammar' are encoded in the terms of pro-nuclear arguments: the other side is 'catching up', 'building up', 'expanding', etc.; one side 'perceives', 'believes', 'knows' that the other is doing so. (He also thinks he knows what the other thinks he knows he thinks ... This is another strange spiral, which enters the calculations of strategists and the rhetoric of politicians.) The outcome is the inculcation of a notion of the arms spiral that we are told is 'logic', and which appears cogent because it is self-contained. The danger is that in reality such cycles and spirals as do exist become unstable and disintegrate, while we are hypnotised by the beautiful simplicity of our conceptualisations.

Many of the cultural symbols which we have seen recycled and pressed into service for the assimilation of the atomic and nuclear experience have this circular quality. Many are ambivalent; they unite contradictory ideas in a single verbal formulation. The animism that produces such symbols is itself paradoxical, in the sense that it seeks the unification of terms that seem opposed: culture and nature. It may be that we cannot accept contraries, but we have ways of so coalescing them that it is difficult to escape the loop that binds them. Once the paradox is inserted, the opposites are kept separate but bound, as in an optical illusion:

> but nature is human
> but nature is not human
> so nature is nature

This is how paradoxical mysteries like the Trinity also work. But what of Oppenheimer's 'Trinity', the atomic explosion itself? To conclude, let us look at some fascinating strange loops that are found in the language of the nuclear age. The sun, as we have seen, was and perhaps is an image with a powerful hold on the human imagination. It is an ambivalent, paradoxical image, since it signifies both life-giving warmth and life-destroying heat:

> but the sun gives life
> but also the sun brings death
> so the sun does not give life

Now if the sun symbol is recycled, as we have seen it is, and used to assimilate the bomb to human experience, then we have something like the following:

> but the bomb = the sun = life
> but the bomb = death
> so the bomb = life

Strange loops also operate in the standard arguments in favour of nuclear weapons; they are perhaps compelling and difficult to answer just because they involve such loops. One such is involved in the argument that 'deterrents' have to be inconceivably destructive, but that in practice they will not destroy because they are too destructive to use, though the enemy must believe that it could and would be used, even though it cannot be used, because it is too destructive to use...

but the deterrent destroys
so the deterrent cannot be used
so the deterrent does not destroy

This type of argument grew out of a period when the horror of the bomb did indeed seem to act as a restraint. As the spiral grows through time, however, its liability to disintegrate – and the tendency to want to escape from it – increases. The danger before us now is that we try to escape from the loop by modifying the second line of the above paradox: that is, by finding ways in which nuclear weapons *can* be used. The hopeful prospect is that the self-sustaining paradoxes of classic deterrence will lose their 'credibility' and oblige us to find a way out. In the late 1980s, that may be what we are seeing.

Notes and References

Chapter 1

1. On the definitions of utopia, eutopia and dystopia cf. Lyman Tower Sargent, *British and American Utopian Literature 1576–1975: An Annotated Bibliography* (G.K. Hall & Co., Boston). On linguistics and science fiction, see W. Meyer, *Aliens and Linguists*. The approach taken in the present paper differs from Meyer's in the way in which linguistics itself is conceived. That is, I do not assume that linguistics is an established science like physics, etc., but rather that it is likely in some of its manifestations (a) to have the quality of myth, and (b) to have an ideological function in particular historical circumstances. On this view cf. Chilton, 'Orwell, Language and Linguistics', *Language and Communication*, Vol. 4, no. 2 (1984), pp. 129–46, and 'Orwell et Saussure: une confrontation', *La Quinzaine Litteraire*, no. 411 (1984), pp. 8–9. A wide-ranging account and discussion of imaginary languages, including those of science fiction, though without the overall political implications which we are concerned to draw out here, is to be found in Marina Yaguello's book, *Les fous du langage: Des langues imaginaires et de leurs inventeurs* (Seuil, 1984).
2. *After Babel* (London, 1975).
3. The notion of language as a closed, thought-determining system holds particular fascination for science fiction writers. Cf. David Harvey's essay, 'The Language of Science' in Michael Moorcock (ed.), *New Worlds: An Anthology*, on artificial philosophical and mathematical systems; this rests on an erroneous analogy between such systems, dominant scientific paradigms and literary styles, all of which he calls 'languages'.
4. J.R. Firth, *The Tongues of Men*, London, 1970 (first edition 1937), Chapter 5. The ideas of this period are well summarised in J. Knowlson, *Universal Language Schemes in England and France, 1600–1800*, University of Toronto Press, Toronto, 1975.
5. *New Atlantis ...* pp. 239, pp. 244–5. On Bacon, science, masculine dominance and the birth of the atomic bomb, see Brian Easlea, *Fathering the Unthinkable. Masculinity, Scientists and the Nuclear Arms Race* (Pluto, 1983).
6. Firth, *Tongues of Men*, p. 64.
7. Wilkins's classifications resemble those of a brand of linguistics known as 'systemic linguistics' and its computer application by Winograd, whose SHRDLU program simulates a 'world' of three-dimensional blocks.

8. *The Collected Essays, Journalism and Letters of George Orwell* (ed. Sonia Orwell and Ian Angus), 4 vols.(London, 1968), Vol. IV, pp. 213/214.
9. Sprat, in his *History of the Royal Society*, speaks of the Society's 'Constant Resolution...to return back to the primitive purity and shortness when men delivered so many things almost in an equal number of words' (quoted in Knowlson, *Universal Language Schemes*, p. 40ff).
10. 'Utopia and Science Fiction', in P. Parrinder (ed.), *Science Fiction: A Critical Guide*, p. 56.
11. *The Coming Race*, p. 231.
12. Cf. *Collected Essays*, Vol. IV, p. 127.
13. Brian Aldiss, *Billion Year Spree* (Weidenfeld and Nicolson, 1973).
14. See *Collected Essays*, Vol. III, pp. 85–6.
15. *Basic English: A General Introduction with Rules of Grammar* (London, 1932; first edition, 1930), pp. 26, 28. Ogden seems to regard inflections as 'linguistic forms and rituals (p. 28), reflecting a non-scientific culture and "word-magic". This is rather difference from Müller's view, but the principle of treating morphological characteristics as symbols of cultural, social or political ones is the same.
16. *Basic English*, p. 20.
17. Cf. the correspondence in the Orwell Archive, University College, London, 6 December 1942; undated, 1942; 17 December 1942. The role of Basic in Orwell's novel is discussed by H. Fink, 'The Epitome of Parody Technique in *Nineteen Eighty-Four*', in *Critical Survey*, 5 (1971).
18. *Basic English*, p. 52.
19. *Nineteen Eighty-Four* (Penguin, 1962), p. 44.
20. *Basic English*, p. 52.
21. See B. Crick, *George Orwell: A Life*.
22. Russell's Introduction to Wittgenstein's *Tractatus Logico-Philosophicus* (London, 1961), p.x. On this, and the relevance to Newspeak of other language-philosophical ideas cf. J. Koberl, 'Der sprachphilosophische Hintergrund von Newspeak', *Arbeiten aus Anglistik und Amerikanistik*, 4 (1979), pp. 171–83.
23. *Collected Essays*, Vol. II, p. 7; cf. also p. 6: 'Yet if the words represented meanings as fully and accurately as height multiplied by the base represents the area of a parellologram, at least the *necessity* for lying would never exist.'
24. *Collected Essays*, Vol. II, p. 9.
25. *Collected Essays*, Vol. II, 11. Cf. Socrates in Plato's *Cratylus*: 'Not every man is able to give a name, but only a master of names; and this is the legislator, who of all skilled artisans in the world is the rarest...only he who looks to the name which each thing by nature has, and is, will be able to express the ideal forms of things in letters and syllables.'
26. *Tongues of Men*, pp. 70–71.
27. *Science and Sanity* (4th ed., Lakevill, Connecticut, 1958), p. 11.
28. *Collected Essays*, Vol. IV, p. 127.
29. Cf. Colin Wilson in E.F. Bleiler (ed.), *Science Fiction Writers* (New York, 1982), p. 215, also explains the confusion as being due to 'the pace of the plot'.
30. *Science and Sanity*, pp. 538–9.
31. It is significant that Meyer (*op. cit.*) dismisses Watson's political statement as 'nineteenth-century', in contrast to his Chomskyan linguistics. Meyer's statement looks like a desire to evade evaluation of Watson's political points.

Chapter 2

1. A more detailed explanation of the ideas behind this formulation is given in Chapter 6.

2. 'Politics and the English Language', *Collected Essays and Journalism*, Vol. 4 (Secker and Warburg, 1968).

3. Ludwig Wittgenstein, *Tractatus Logico-Philosophicus*; Ferdinand de Saussure, *Cours de linguistique générale*; cf. above Chapter 1, and on Saussure and Orwell, P. Chilton, 'Orwell et Saussure: une confrontation', *La Quinzaine littéraire*, No. 4111 (1984). The edition of Saussure referred to below is *Cours de linguistique générale*, (ed. T. de Mauro; Geneva, 1973).

4. See Carl Freedman, 'Writing, Ideology and Politics: Orwell's "Politics and the English language" and English Composition', *College English*, Vol. 43, No. 4 (April 1981).

5. This point was made for reified conceptions of *la langue* by V.N. Volosinov, *Marxism and the Philosophy of Language* (first Russian edition, 1929). For a detailed summary and critique of Volosinov, see T. Pateman, 'Discourse in Life', *UEA Papers in Linguistics*, pp. 16–17 (1982).

6. Cf. R. Harris, 'Language and Speech' in R. Harris (ed.), *Approaches to Language* (Pergamon Press, 1983).

7. Cf. N. Chomsky, *Aspects of the Theory of Syntax* (MIT Press, 1965), p. 8–10.

8. T. Pateman, 'From Nativism to Sociolinguistics: Integrating a Theory of Language Growth, with a Theory of Speech Practices', *Journal for the Theory of Social Behaviour*, 1985.

9. Cf. P. Chilton, 'Autonomy and Paradox in Literary Theory' in *Journal of Literary Semantics* XII/I (1983); also B. Torode and Silverman, *The Material Word*, and F. Lentricchia, *After the New Criticism* (1980).

10. G. Sampson in *Liberty and Language* (O.U.P., 1979) attacks Chomsky's linguistics as a reflection of an underlying collectivism. His own linguistics has the dubious merit of acknowledging its basis in Thatcherite economics and social attitudes: cf. the critical reviews by D. Lightfoot in *Journal of Linguistics*, XVII, 1 (1981). As an example of what a New Right Linguistics might look like, cf. Sampson's 'The Economics of Conversation' in N.V. Smith (ed.), *Mutual Knowledge*, Academic Press (1982), which is based on an analogy derived from the economics of Hayek – and for a critique of Hayek, cf. Orwell himself, *Collected Essays*, Vol. 3, pp. 117–18.

11. D. Hymes, *On Communicative Competence* (1971), excerpted in J.B. Pride and J. Holmes (ed.), *Sociolinguistics* (Penguin, 1972). I consider here Habermas's early 'Towards a Theory of Communicative Competence', in P. Dreitzel (ed.), *Recent Sociology No. 2: Patterns of Communicative Behaviour* (Macmillan, 1970), rather than 'What Is Universal Pragmatics?' in his *Communication and the Evolution of Society* (Heinemann, 1979), because it permits a particularly clear contrast between the two notions of 'communicative competence'.

12. See, for instance, D. Spender, *Man-Made Language* (Routledge and Kegan Paul, 1985); Thorn and Henley (eds.), *Language and Sex: Difference and Dominance* (Newburg House, 1975).

13. Hymes in Pride and Holmes (eds.), p. 277.

14. Habermas in Dreitzel (ed.), p. 144.

15. Habermas, *op. cit.*, p. 134.

16. *Ibid.*, p. 138.

17.   *Ibid.*, p. 141
18.   *Ibid.*, p. 143.
19.   *Ibid.*, p. 144.

Chapter 4

1.   B. Bernstein, *Class, Codes and Control* (Routledge and Kegan Paul, 1971).
2.   Roger Fowler and Bob Hodge, 'Orwellian linguistics' in R. Fowler, *et al.* (eds.), *Language and Control*, (Routledge and Kegan Paul, 1979).
3.   M. Edelman, *Political Language. Words that Succeed and Policies that Fail* (New York, Academic Press, 1977), Chapter 6.
4.   Cf., for instance, W. Labov, 'The logic of non-standard English' in P. Giglioli, (ed.), *Language and Social Context* (Penguin, 1972).
5.   M. Edelman, *Political Language* p. 109.
6.   C.L. Lerman, 'Dominant discourse: the institutional voice and control of topic' in H. Davis, and P. Walton, *Language, Image, Media* (Blackwell, 1983).
7.   *Nineteen Eighty-Four* (Penguin, 1962), p. 44, p. 45.
8.   Quoted by Lerman 'Dominant discourse', p. 99.
9.   *Nineteen Eighty-Four*, p. 161.
10.   Cf. Chapter 5 below and, on analysing metaphors, Chapter 7.

Chapter 5

1.   E.P. Thompson, *Protest and Survive* (ed. E.P. Thompson and Dan Smith; Penguin Books, 1980), p. 51.
2.   *Ibid.*, p. 50.
3.   P.H. Vigor, 'The semantics of deterrence and defense', in *Soviet Naval Policy: Objectives and Constraints* (ed. M. MacGwire, K. Booth and J. McDonnell; Praeger, 1975), pp. 471–6.
4.   I am grateful to Mark Harrison for some of these points.
5.   Cf. E. Rosch, 'Linguistic relativity', in P. Johnson-Laird and P. Wason (eds.), *Thinking* (C.U.P., 1977).
6.   G.A. Miller, 'Psychology, language and levels of communication'.
7.   I am using remarks made by T. Pateman, 'Power *over* language and power *in* language', but not attempting here to follow up the theoretical issues raised.
8.   Dwight Bollinger, *Language. The Loaded Weapon. The Use and Abuse of Language Today* (Longman, 1980), p. 22.
9.   On this cf. Roger Fowler and Tim Marshall, 'The war against peacemongering' in Chilton (ed.), *Language and the Nuclear Arms Debate* (Pinter, 1985).
10.   Paul Rogers, *A Guide to Nuclear Weapons*, Peace Studies Papers, Number 5 (Housmans, London, 1981), p.5.
11.   cf. Pateman, 'Power *over* language'.

Chapter 6

1.   M.L. Minsky, 'A framework for representing knowledge' excerpted in D. Metzing (ed.), *Frame Conceptions and Text Understanding* (De Gruyter, 1980), p. 7.
2.   Ibid. p. 9.

3. R.P. Abelson, 'The structure of belief systems', in R.C. Schantz and K.M. Colby (eds.), *Computer Modes of Thought and Language* (W.H. Freeman, 1973); R.C. Schank and R. Abelson, *Scripts, Goals, Plans and Understanding* (Erlbaum, 1976).
4. Schank and Abelson, *Scripts, Goals, Plans and Understanding*, p. 40.
5. See Abelson, 'The structure of belief systems', and W. Downes, *Language and Society* (Fontana, 1984).
6. Cf. D. Hofstadter, *Gödel, Escher, Bach* (Penguin, 1980). John Searle, *Minds, Brains and Science: The 1984 Reith lectures* (BBC, 1984).
7. Gigantomachies – battle between gods and giants – play a major role in our Jewish, Greek, Roman and Germanic cultural inheritance. There are connections also with apocalyptic myths that are of direct relevance to cold war ideological themes considered here. Gog and Magog, giants in some folklore traditions, are, interestingly enough, collective names in medieval writing for savage cannibalistic tribes of the North, followers of the Antichrist who spread terror and devastation only to be annihilated by a mighty messianic emperor in the Last Days. Cf. N. Cohn, *The Pursuit of the Millenium* (Paladin, 1970), p. 29ff, 78,, who also tellingly remarks: 'Invasion or the threat of invasion by Huns, Magyars, Mongols, Saracens or Turks always stirred memories of those hordes of Antichrist, the people of Gog and Magog' (p. 35). The fear, unjustified or justified, of Russian hordes from the North seems to evoke similar fantasies. Jerry Falwell, the spiritual confidant of President Reagan, believes that the biblical account of the Apocalypse predicts nuclear holocaust. My point is that these myths, scripts or frames are well entrenched and have a life of their own: they have nothing to do with the actual problem of the Soviet Union. A further point about giant figures in cold war mythology could be made within a Freudian and Lacanian framework: the giant is the threatening father of infantile fantasies, the Other who, mirrored in the self, is an obsessive threat to autonomy. The point again is that this has nothing to do with the political problem of the Soviet Union and the United States, though the psychological potency of the imagery in the Western psyche may explain the hold of the ideology of the permanent enemy, the Threat, the Other. For a Lacanian approach to the doctrine of deterrence, see P. Claes and W. Van Belle in Chilton (ed.), *Language and the Nuclear Arms Debate*.
8. *Rhetoric*, III, 1410b.
9. Chicago University Press, 1980.
10. *Metaphors We Live By*, pp. 156–7.
11. J.R. Hobbs, 'Metaphor interpretation as selective inferencing', *Proceedings of the Seventh Joint International Conference on Artificial Intelligence* (1981) pp. 85–91).
12. Hobbs, 'Metaphor...', p. 90.
13. S. Hillgartner, R.C. Bell and R. O'Connor, *Nukespeak: The Selling of Nuclear Technology in America* (Penguin, 1983).
14. Quoted in *Bulletin of Atomic Scientists*, xxx, 9 (1974), p. 20.
15. Statement made in 1972, quoted by Irene Matthews (pseudonym), 'Death of a plutonium worker', in *Unsolved*, Vol. IV, no. 48, p. 951.
16. Text quoted by G. Hook, 'The nuclearization of language', *Journal of Peace Research*, 21 3 (1983).
17. See the Russell-Einstein Manifesto of 1955.

Chapter 7

1. Cf. Bloom, A., The Linguistic Shaping of Thought (Erlbaum, 1981).
2. Cf. Bollinger, D., *Language: The Loaded Weapon* (Longman 1980), 61ff.
3. For a general treatment of the media's construction of the Falklands war, see Robert Harn's *Gotcha! The Media, the Government and the Falklands Crisis* (Faber, 1983).
4. Salman Rushdie on E.P. Thompson's *Guardian* article of 31 May 1982; reproduced in E.P. Thompson's *The Heavy Dancers* (Merlin Press, 1985), p. 5.
5. For a fuller discussion of metaphor, see above, Chapter 6.
6. *Daily Mail*, 19 July 1982.
7. Cf. Bollinger, *Language*, p. 62, p. 143.
8. *Daily Mail*, 3 May 1982.
9. *Daily Express*, 11 May 1982.
10. *Sunday Telegraph*, 20 June 1982.
11. *Sunday Telegraph*, 12 July 1982.
12. This quotation is used by J.B. Thompson, *Studies in the Theory of Ideology* (Polity, 1984), as an example of what he terms 'the mobilization of meaning', which he considers sustains relations of domination by legitimating, dissimulating or reifying an existing state of affairs.
13. *Sunday Times*, 4 July 1982, reporting the Prime Minister's words.
14. *Times*, 5 July 1982.
15. *Sunday Telegraph*, 17 June 1982.
16. 19 July 1982.
17. 19 July 1982.
18. Carter's metaphor is discussed by Lakoff and Johnson in *Metaphors We Live By*; cf. above, p. 61.

Chapter 8

1. *The Times*, 7 August 1945, 4; 10 August 1945, p. 4, my italics.
2. E.P. Thompson and Dan Smith (eds.), *Protest and Survive* (Penguin, 1980), p. 51.
3. *Nineteen Eighty-Four* (Penguin, 1970), p. 241.
4. See B.L. Whorf, *Language, Thought and Reality*, (ed. J.B. Carroll; Cambridge, Mass; 1956); cf. above, Chapter 4.
5. *Language and Responsibility* (The Harvester Press, 1979), p. 38.
6. 'Politics and the English Language', *The Collected Essays, Journalism and Letters of George Orwell*, Vol. 4, 166.
7. Herbert Marcuse, *One Dimensional Man* (Sphere Books, 1968), Chapter 4, 'The closing of the universe of discourse'. The semantics of the words *deter, deterrent*, and *deterrence* is discussed in detail in Chilton (ed.), *Language and the Nuclear Arms Debate* (Pinter, 1985).
8. *The Times*, 8 August 1945, p. 5.
9. *The Times*, 10 August 1945, p. 5.
10. *The Times*, 7 August 1945, p. 4.
11. The above paragraphs were originally read as a paper at the Institute of Contemporary Arts, London, on Hiroshima day, 1981, and were reprinted in *Sanity* (No. 5, 1978), the journal of the British Campaign for Nuclear Disarmament.
12. For this approach to metaphor cf. G. Lakoff, and M. Johnson, *Metaphors We*

Live By, and above, Chapter 6.

13. Note that in January 1984 the Soviet negotiator at the (by then defunct) Geneva talks claimed that a proposal had in fact been made in November 1983 which included British and French nuclear forces, and that West German leaks had undermined progress. The US negotiator has denied this, as have the White House and the West Germans (cf. *Guardian*, 13 January 1984).

14. V. Osgood, C., 'Psycho-social dynamics and the prospects for mankind', lecture to the Peace Science Society, 1977, and to UN colloquium, 1978.

15. Osgood, 'Psycho-social dynamics,' p. 22. Orwell too comments on problems caused by negatives in his essay 'Politics and the English language'.

16. I.L. Janis, *Victims of Groupthink*, quoted by M. Edelman, *Political Language* (Academic Press, 1977), p. 194.

17. George Ball, *New York Review of Books*, 8 November 1984.

18. The politics of the actual situation are discussed with finesse by E.P. Thompson in *Double Exposure*, Merlin Press 1985. What I seek to do in the present paragraphs is to outline the way in which pragmatics (the discipline within language studies concerned with the situated practices of language use) can contribute to a grasp of what is going on in such situations in general.

19. Osgood, 'Psycho-social dynamics', p. 3.

20. Cf. Osgood, 'Psycho-social dynamics', p. 6.

21. Cf. D.M. Kaplan and A. Schwerner, *The Domesday Dictionary*, Cape, 1964, p. 75.

22. Sections II and III of this chapter were given as part of an invited talk to the Peace Pledge Union in October 1983.

Chapter 9

1. Cf. P. Chilton, (ed), *Language and the Nuclear Arms Debate*, (Pinter 1985), 104, and above, Chapter 5.

2. I am grateful to Donna Gregory, MacArthur fellow at the Center for International and Stategic Affairs, Los Angeles, for drawing these points concerning Kahn to my attention.

3. Cf. A. Rapoport, 'Verbal maps and global politics', *Etcetera*, 37 (1980), pp. 297–313.

4. E.g. 'Psycho-social dynamics and the prospects for mankind' (lecture to UN colloquium, 1978), 'Conservative words and radical sentences in the semantics of international politics', *Studies in the Linguistic Sciences*, 8 (1979), 'Reciprocal initiative', in *The Liberal Papers*, (ed. J. Roosevelt; New York, 1962).

5. Habermas's concept of the 'ideal communication situation' is instructive in this regard, as is Bourdieu's notion of 'symbolic violence'.

6. See M.J. Reddy, 'The conduit metaphor', in Ortony, A. (ed.), *Metaphor and Thought* (C.U.P., 1979).

7. cf. G. Leech, *The Principles of Pragmatics* (Arnold, 1983).

8. But cf. W. Van Belle and P. Claes, 'The logic of deterrence' in Chilton (1985).

9. On this interpretation of negatives, cf. Leech (1983).

10. cf. P. Brown and S. Levinson, 'Universals in language usage: politeness phenomena' in E.N. Goody (ed.), *Questions & Politeness*, (C.U.P. 1978), and Leech (1983).

11. Malinowski, B., *Argonauts of the Western Pacific* (Routledge, 1932), is cited on this point by Franck and Weisband. There is now important work on the linguistic

management of face-threatening acts, including offers, proposals, invitations etc. Cf. E. Goffman, *Interaction Ritual* (1967); P. Brown and S. Levinson, 'Universals in language usage' in E. Goody (ed.), Question and Politeness: Strategies in Social Interaction (CUP, 1978), G. Leech, *Principles of Pragmatics* (1983).

Chapter 10

1. Jacques Monod, *Chance and Necessity* (Collins, 1972), p. 38.
2. The process is not entirely new – something similar happened when gunpowder and guns were produced. Indeed, something similar happens whenever more 'primitive' cultures confront technologically advanced ones: e.g. American Indian reactions to Spanish armour and horses; the Cargo cult.
3. Humphrey, *Listener* (29 October, 1981), p. 494.
4. M. Mandelbaum, *The Nuclear Revolution* pp. 29–40. He makes use of Mary Douglas, *Purity and Danger* (Penguin, 1966).
5. Monod, *Chance and Necessity*, 155.
6. *Ibid*, p. 154.
7. *Ibid*, p. 159. The second type is illustrated, incidentally, in the *Daily Worker*'s view of the bomb, discussed above.
8. Professor George Kennan, Former US Ambassador to Russia, quoted by Humphrey, who uses the rabbit image.
9. Douglas Hofstadter's *Gödel, Escher, Bach* is in itself a monument to the fascination of the paradox, and goes some way towards explaining this fascination in terms of information processing and human biology.
10. Mandelbaum, *Nuclear Revolution*, p. 116.

Index

DATE DUE

JAN 0 2 1992			
MAY 0 9 1995			
JUL 0 7 2003			
12/20			

DEMCO 38-297